Murdered by A Christian, On a *Sunday*

By
Bianca Smith

© 2018 Bianca Smith

This book is a work of non-fiction.

ISBN: 0692141138

ISBN-13: 978-0692141137

All rights reserved. No part of this book may be reproduced in any written, electronic, recording, or photocopying without written permission of the author. The only exception is brief quotations in printed reviews.

In loving memory of my big brother, Fabian "Fabe" Smith.
January 16, 1988~February 19, 2017

I never knew what it meant to live until you died.
You have won your race; watch over me while I run mine.
FABE: Forget Average Be Extraordinary
Your life will be celebrated, I promise.
-Bianca Smith

Acknowledgements

Prelude

I	First 48……………………………………..1	
II	The Criminal (in)Justice System…………18	
III	Good Grief………………………………31	
IV	Is This What You Called Me For?………..44	
V	#FABE………………………………..…..49	
VI	Trial……………………………………….59	
VII	Church Hurt……………………………...77	
VIII	Life After Death………………………….85	

Appendices

    Kubler-Ross Grief Cycle

    Victim Impact Statement

About the Author

Murdered by A Christian, On a *Sunday*

Acknowledgements

This book was birthed from pain and doubt. I am forever indebted to those who were sure of my abilities during a season when I was not. To my parents: thank you. You loved me when you did not understand me. I could not ask for more. To my Great-Grandmama and late Grandma, Catherine and Rosie, thank you for raising me and my teenage parents. Grandmama, you introduced me to the Father, the Son, and the Holy Spirit. To the rest of my family and surviving siblings, thank you for being that village. A special expression of gratitude to my uncle, F. Robinson. When I mentioned writing a book and launching a business, you responded, "I hope this isn't a scam." Despite your skepticism, you helped fund both projects.

I would like to acknowledge the first friend I made when I moved to Houston, Trenee Green. I was so overwhelmed with Houston, but you and your family had a small-town vibe. For ten years, I called you when I could not find my way home. When my brother was murdered, I called you when I could not find myself. I am also thankful for my church, graduate cohort, and FABE supporters.

Justice and the victory that fills the pages of this book would have been impossible without the work of Prosecutor K. Forcht, Homicide Detective B. Davis, and every juror who served to convict Tyler Christian Green of first-degree murder.

Several game-changers have invested their time and resources into my professional growth and development: Anthony Graves, Dr. D. Pooler, and the full-time and adjunct professors at Baylor University's Houston Campus. I hope I have made my mentors proud.

I am alive at a time when the status of women is changing forever. We are no longer concerned about the glass ceiling. We're shattering it and unapologetically slaying on the broken pieces. Here's just a few of the women who inspire me most: Oprah Winfrey, Angela Rye, and Lakeisha Gatlin. Alethea Wren and Tameko Clayton: You are the epitome of a Mother. You have shared stories about how your lives were drastically changed by the lives of your first born, your sons. The enemy has consistently attacked you through your children, but you never surrendered. You queens have taught me how to smile even when I'm hurting.

Whoever you are, wherever you are, I wrote this book for you. I hope my transparency regarding the bondage of pain helps set you free. Thank you for even reading this far into my story.

Sincere gratitude flows from the pieces of my broken heart....

-Bianca Smith

Prelude

I'm a Christian. In the past, when someone lost a loved one, like an email [Auto-Reply], I'd respond, "He/she's in a better place now," "Heaven has gained another angel," "I know how you feel," "I know what you're going through," or, the one that took the least amount of thought, "Just pray about it." My own pain has made me more sensitive to the pain of others; I pray that I think first, and never use any of those phrases again. I pray that my response is a sincere expression of sympathy and empathy, not merely a result of habit.
    -Amen

I.   First 48

On February 14, 2017, I worked a majority of the day. After fighting with the ungodly traffic in Houston, I made it home. Fabe was already there, as usual. We both tried to hide the depression of yet another Valentine's Day and no Valentine. I pretended to be so busy that I had barely noticed what day it was, and Fabe pretended that he'd rather dance in and out of uncommitted relationships than settle down. Even when I was in "situationships" that called for me to go on a date for a few hours of the day, Fabe and I always spent Valentine's Day together. The situationships were…distractions. They looked like relationships but lacked the benefits. I was better off with my brother.

We laughed and joked about how no one wanted either of us. He'd go so far as to say, "It's just gon' be me and you forever. No kids. I'm not gon' have a wife. You not gon' have a husband. We gon' be right here, together." I would usually respond by begging him to retract his statements and not speak negatively over my life. This day was no different. Fabe said, "Ay, I got you some cookies!" I replied, "Thanks, but they don't fit my meal plan." Like most people I knew, I was still within 45 days of the new year, so I had not totally disregarded my resolutions. With both sarcasm and sympathy, Fabe said, "Girl, you ain't got no man. Just eat the cookies." I laughed a little, but the reality of that statement was heavier than the calories those cookies were packing. So, I clapped back. I teased him about being a year older than me, and having counseled several women through their relationship problems, as if they would leave their spouse for him. Once he and I got started in a roasting session, it could go all night. And I do mean ALL night. He would leave, think of something, and call me just to fire back. He would send me screenshots and direct messages (DMs) just to fire back. I escaped this session easily, though.

Murdered by a Christian, On a Sunday

It was Tuesday, and Fabe knew I had Bible Study. I invited him to Bible Study and he declined. He said, "Oh no, y'all First Lady too fine. I can't focus in there." We laughed, and I told him how much more he needed God to intervene in his life. But, I appreciated his transparency; it could not be matched. He had a way of sharing his thoughts and feelings that made me feel obligated to do the same.

The next day, I received an email confirming my acceptance into a Graduate Program at Baylor University- a school that I had never dreamed of applying to before meeting one of my mentors. I was born into poverty to teenage parents along the coast of Mississippi. I like to say that my parents and I grew up together. According to NBC News, in 2009, Mississippi ranked highest in the nation for the highest teenage birthrate[1]. Mississippi has also consistently ranked one of the lowest states in the nation for quality of public school education. I managed to graduate high school and my parents were not yet grandparents. I was no better than anyone, but I was different. I had a pair of praying great-grandmothers. And when they prayed, I saw circumstances change. So, I prayed before I opened the email from Baylor's Office of Admissions. I had already claimed it. I was so enthusiastic, but I knew who would be even more excited about this next chapter of my life. Fabe loved to receive and share news like that. I have overheard him brag about accomplishments that I have never even mentioned to others. Somehow, I called my mom and shared the news, but never called Fabe.

Maybe I got distracted. The very next day, Thursday February 16, 2017, I received the call that my first nephew was born. Fabe and I were extremely excited. I started to plan a trip home to Mississippi. I wanted to surprise my sister,

---

[1] http://www.nbcnews.com/id/28538524/ns/health-childrens_health/t/mississippi-now-has-highest-teen-birth-rate/#.Wsv5DYjwZPY)

First 48

because I felt terrible about having missed the baby shower. I told Fabe to be ready to head home that Friday, giving us both about 48 hours to prepare. I knew I would be exhausted from a week's work but still eager to meet this addition to the family. I knew that no matter what, Fabe would be ready. And, he was one of the few people I trusted to drive me on the highway at night.

Well, Friday came. Understandably, Fabe decided that joining me was not a good economic decision because his car was being repaired. Although so many elements of this trip were outside of my comfort zone, I went home. Fabe called every hour to check on me. Most of the calls lasted 3-5 minutes because he did not want to distract me. Although brief, he never ended a call without telling me that he loved me. I don't know why he felt the need to say it so often. I already knew that, and he knew that I knew that. He called around 1:30 AM and was relieved that I had made it to Mississippi safely. He enjoyed the pictures of the baby. Our nephew was 8 pounds, pale, and had curly dark brown hair blooming from his scalp like flowers. Fabe was hyped! He mentioned that he had just left the studio recording new music. He asked about the family, and they all asked about him. My life was pretty boring, so my distant family and I usually bonded over stories that involved Fabe. I could not wait to tell them how Fabe, in preparation for a job interview, decided to recycle one of my dad's old brief cases. I was impressed! After his interview, he bragged about having swept the managers off their feet. Amid our conversation and his celebratory dance, the brief case swung open. His legal pad filled with rap lyrics fell out. I am not sure if he interviewed or freestyled, but his talent and vibrant personality secured the job.

The time with my family and calls with Fabe on speakerphone kept me so busy. I was home less than 48 hours, but I had to return to Houston. On Sunday, February 19, 2017, I hit the highway around 5 AM. I knew Avis rental car company closed early on Sundays, and I did not want to pay any extra fees for the car that I was driving.

By 11:00 AM, I was within a mile of my subdivision. I called Fabe's cell phone, so he would be prepared to follow me to return the rental car, but he did not answer. I did not call again, because I was very close. Soon after, my mom called to check on me. I told her that I was really close to home and needed someone to follow me to Avis. She told me she was not home, but Fabe was. She warned me that he was asleep when she left, but she would try and wake him up for me.

Because I did not have my original set of keys, only the rental car keys, I had to knock and ring the doorbell a few times. I became agitated because I needed to go to the restroom. Fabe apologized for taking longer than usual to answer the door. We discussed my time with family, traffic, and the weather. The conversation was rushed as I was trying to quickly visit the restroom and get my car keys. I needed to return that rental car! I told Fabe that I needed him to follow me. I said, "Hurry, get your shoes on. I gotta get to Avis before they close at noon or 1, and I have a meeting." I often referred to my volunteering as "meetings," because my family had given me a few responses in the past that I did not know how to interpret. In their defense, I did not know how to articulate that some of my volunteer work was more fulfilling than anything I had ever been paid to do. I should have explained to them that as a state employee, a career choice that they were fond of, I was required to do lots of pro bono work. It was disguised within my salary. My family often responded as if I was doing too much. They said things like, "I don't know how you do that," and "You're ripping and running too much." Despite the lack of understanding, I knew my mom's comments were rooted in love because she would also say, "you need to get some rest." I learned that if I said "meeting" and made it sound work related, the responses were different. My parents worked really hard to be inducted into the middle-class tax bracket. Somewhere along the way, they adopted the belief that long hours, salaried positions, and health insurance that one can barely afford is a depiction of success. If my busyness was perceived as a requirement for my job, they did not probe for any other information. That was their normal.

In my haste to get to Avis, I could see Fabe in my peripheral. He was standing in the hallway, looking into the mirror, and twisting strands of his hair. He was excited about a new kiwi lime moisturizer he purchased and wanted me to smell it. I quickly replied, "Mmmm, yes! Smells good, but let's go!" He followed me downstairs and realized he did not have on any shoes. He must have heard my deep breathing, so instead of returning upstairs for his shoes, he put on a pair of my slippers. My slippers were a size 6.5, and Fabe wore a size 9. I did not have time to address the discrepancy. Besides, I wore his stuff all the time.

We tailgated to Avis. He drove my car, and I drove the rental car. Avis is about five miles from our home, and traffic was very light. He waited patiently while I went inside to return the keys. When I opened the door of my car to put my luggage in, Fabe said, 'I'll drive. I know you probably tired." Feeling relieved, I replied, "Yes." Although I knew I could be transparent with my brother, I also knew that he thought so much of me. So, I often pretended to be stronger than I really was. I was exhausted. Within 48 hours, I drove more hours than I slept. Still hyped about his Friday night studio session, Fabe offered to play his new song for me. I looked at my phone, and I pretended to be focused on something else. I acted as though I had not heard his offer. He was persistent about connecting his phone to my auxiliary cord. I told him "No, I don't wanna hear it today, because it's Sunday and I know you're probably cussin'." He looked over at me in the passenger seat, gave a really big smile, and connected it anyway. That smile had gotten so much out of me over the years. I made no attempt to listen to the words, but I really enjoyed the rhythm. I told him I liked the song almost immediately. I thought, "the quicker I provide approval, the quicker he'll turn it off." We continued to talk about family, how much our younger siblings and cousins had grown, and he asked about our grandparents. Momo and Papa were his favorites. For ten years, Fabe was their only grandson. I interrupted our conversation by telling him I needed to return to Avis for my phone charger, but he insisted that he had one in his car that I could have.

He pulled into the driveway. I walked in the house and left the front door open for him. He walked up the driveway and stated, "I'll be right back, you can lock the door." I turned around, and at that point, all I could see was his back. For a few seconds, I watched as he walked to his car on his tip toes. Fabe had a very distinct walk and small frame that fit perfectly with his happy-go-lucky personality.

Later that day, I was scheduled to volunteer with my church's prison ministry at Texas Department of Criminal Justice's Jester III Unit. The unit is over an hour drive from my home, so I knew I needed to get going. I really enjoyed volunteering, but it was not easy. Most times, my efforts required resources that were already scarce, such as time and money. Nevertheless, I always trusted that God would reward me for my service to his people. Once myself and the other church volunteers arrived at the unit, to preserve the battery, I turned my phone off. I had so many issues, and I was not sure if it was the phone, the battery, or the car charger. Once we were granted access onto the unit, we went into the chapel. Despite having been in a correctional facility countless number of times as a staff member, I was still nervous. I was even more nervous because I understood the unwritten rules. I had been exposed to the prison environment beyond the chapel, trustees, and model inmates. So even while being cordial and sharing the goodness of God, I never underestimated the importance of awareness on the prison grounds. I had an immense amount of respect for the offenders who appeared to be seeking a genuine worship experience, but it was obvious that some offenders entered the chapel with their own agenda. Chapel was an opportunity to exit the overcrowded housing areas, see and smell glimpses of the free world, and receive charitable donations…or contraband.

I remember feeling very sick and not being able to sit upright. Sitting on the edge of my seat with my elbows pressed into my knees, I was hoping that I did not make the person sitting behind me nervous or think I was weird. Just as I was not a stranger to the prison environment, I was also used to worshipping in discomfort. I knew how to lift my hands and offer the Lord my Hallelujah when I was hurting, sick, or just did not feel like it. That evening, several inmates dedicated their lives to Christ. I looked out and thought "these could be my brothers, my dad, my uncles, or my cousins." And I quickly remembered that they were my brothers in Christ. I realized early in my criminal justice career that grace was the only reason I was not and had not ever been locked up. It had nothing to do with me or my works.

I became impatient. I was ready to go. I was hungry and thirsty. The inmates offered us water, but I declined a bottle. I always check to make sure the seal had not been broken, but this time, I wanted out of the facility to get my own water. I prayed to God and apologized for my intolerance. I apologized for not giving Him my undivided attention. I wanted Him to know that I was not rushing to get out of His presence. I just needed to get out of there, so I would have access to medicine and food. I was no longer concerned with the inmates and their spiritual needs. Suddenly, and easily, I prioritized my fleshly desires. After waiting for correctional officers to clear count and all offenders to exit the chapel, we were finally freed. We cracked a few jokes about being in there for so many hours and being hungry. I overheard someone say it was almost

9:00 PM. I proceeded down the country road that lead to the prison and turned my cellphone back on. I kept my eyes planted on the road knowing I could easily get lost in this rather unfamiliar rural area. As my phone was restarting, the notification sounds seemed never ending. I looked at my phone and saw missed calls, voice messages, and Instagram notifications. My status bar was filled from left to right. Then, my mom called. I did not really want to tell her that I was just leaving the prison, having volunteered for hours, and was now feeling sick. She also would not have approved of me being an hour away from home at 9:00 PM and having to work the next day. She loves me; she worries about me. I never turn my phone off, but there was no point in leaving it on since I was prohibited from taking it into the prison.

Foolishly, before answering or returning my mom's calls or reading my messages, I checked my DMs on Instagram. An old high school buddy sent me a message. The message nearly covered my entire screen. The first sentence read, **"I'm sorry you found your brother dead."** I thought. "She's weird. She doesn't know what she's talking about." I remember frowning a little and thinking that some people are so rude! Was this one of those stupid chain messages that instruct you to forward the message to 20 people to avoid something bad? I love to laugh and employ my sense of humor, but death was not something to joke about. Who would just make up something about somebody being dead? I remember thinking, "Ugh, social media is not good for me." I closed the message without replying. I was agitated with her. She and I had only spoken once within the past two years, but she knew how I felt about my brother. I had several other DMs, but I did not open them. My agitation led to an ebonic spasm. I threw up my hand and said to myself, "They ain't talking bout nutn." I had yet to call my mom back or return any of the other missed calls, but I started scanning my text messages.

I read several messages that indicated something was terribly wrong. I tried to remain calm; I clearly heard my brother's voice say, "They lie'n! They said Boosie was dead." I believed that voice. Boosie was one of his favorite rappers, and he was right. There had been several rumors about Boosie being dead. Not my brother! No way! We had not experienced a young, premature, or unexpected death in my family. Besides, God had always prepared me... prepared my family...for loss.

Before I responded to anyone, I needed to plead my case with God first. I screamed to the top of my lungs. I begged God to let it all be a rumor. Within moments, the hypocrite in me was unleashed. I screamed and cried out to God, questioning how He could take my brother after I had sat in a prison for hours serving somebody else's. I was pissed. But at my core, I knew that life would never be the same for me. I knew that the God I serve never took more than He gave and that if He took my brother, I could not imagine what He was about to give me. But at that moment, all I wanted was my brother! My phone died, so I connected it to the charger. Based on past experiences, I knew that I could drive one hour before the battery even reached 10%. I needed answers, so I pulled over to a gas station. I frantically asked to use a telephone, but the clerk refused. He pissed me off, but looking back, he probably had not received that request in years. I returned to my car and realized that I was lost, but I kept driving because my cell phone needed the power to charge. I finally got my phone back on. I called the assistant ministry leader and asked if someone would please help me get home. I was lost and could not access my GPS, because my phone kept dying. In the wake of pain, crying, panting for air, and the groaning in my soul, I tried to tell her that something had happened to my brother, and I feared driving in the rain.

    The assistant ministry leader, driven by her son in a large SUV, met me at a gas station located on a feeder road. I followed them to Beltway 8 which was their exit. For the duration of my trip, I continued praying, screaming, and crying. I still had not returned my mom's call, but I called my sister and her husband. My brother-in-law prayed for me; I did not give him time to say much more. I was praying that somebody would have more favor with God than I did to make this all go away! I called my Aunt Pookie. I could hear pain and sorrow in her voice, so I knew something was true. That was not what I wanted to hear, so I ended that call quickly. I called Kim, an old family friend, and asked her to please go and check on my mom. I sent her into a panic, and then I could barely get the words out to explain what appeared to be wrong. I received a call from a guy back home in Mississippi. He told me he was sorry for my loss, and I told him that I did not even know what was going on yet. I told him that I had been in a meeting and ended that call as quickly as I could. Everyone who called me that night knew that my brother and I shared a very special bond.

It started to rain. Talk about, when it rains it pours. My mom called.

Mom: Bianca
Me: Hello (I could hear in her voice that something was wrong. Real wrong.)
Mom: It's Fabian
Me: (I screamed. Shit got real. My mom did not play like that. She did not forward chain messages, and she knew how I felt about my brother.).
Mom: Bianca, where are you? Please be careful. I'm coming to get you.
Me: I have to go because my phone is gonna die.

(Whenever I took a break from screaming, I could hear my mom crying. It sounded like a helpless cry, much different than my cry which was filled with anger.)
"NNOOO! NNOOO! NNNOOo! Nnooo! Noo! I screamed. (Even while typing this, I can feel the pain, hear my cry, and see this nightmare all over again.) I was gasping for air, experiencing shortness of breath, and choking. I was making myself sick. The last thing I was worried about was choking to death, seizing, or dying from extreme levels of anxiety. I was pissed with God. I was so mad. If I could have, I would have stood toe to toe with Him. I kept screaming. NOOo! My thoughts were all over the place. This ain't right. There's no way my brother can be dead. This cannot be true. They cannot be telling the truth. This 1-hour drive felt like a 72-hour drive. I felt as if I would never get home.

This marked the beginning of the debate between God and me. Before this night, I had never been one to claim "God told me___" or that I heard God speak directly to me. In the midst of my outrage, I said "God, how could you take my brother while I was inside a prison, ministering to somebody else's brother?

God responded, "I thought you said you would serve me until you die?"
Uhoh. I was questioning God! He was questioning me! I humbly admit that, of course, God won the debate. But, that did not prevent me from more questioning and more blaming.
God also continued with the questions, "So, you meant you would serve me until you die ONLY if you didn't have to give up anything? And this was the first day of a very difficult season of my life.

    I finally made it home. I saw Kim's car parked along the street. My brother's car was not home. The likelihood of this being a rumor was decreasing by the second. I walked in to find my parents, two family friends, and one of my brother's acquaintances. One of our family friends was also dealing with the very fresh death of her own sister. When I saw my brother's acquaintance, I felt even more weak. He had bragged about giving my brother drugs before, so I disproved of their friendship. I had not seen him in several months and did not know whether he and my brother were still friends, so I was wondering where he had come from and how he made it to my parent's house before I did. His name is ___. (Fill in the blanks. We all have/had a friend whose loyalty is questionable.) I took a seat on the stairs where I continued gasping for air. I knew in my heart that even if no one else in the room knew, he (___ again) knew what had happened to my brother. I could not stand to look at his face, but I also could not make it past the stairs. I remember struggling to breath and talk. My mom came over and held me. When my mom realized that I could not speak and was fighting to breath, she asked, "Where is your inhaler?" I mouthed a few words, but I did not know the answer to her question. I heard her scream to my sister upstairs, "Look in Bianca's room for her inhaler!" I pressed my elbows into my knees and dropped my head into my hands. This was a damn nightmare. It seemed real because I was really home, and this was really my family. But some elements still seemed unreal. Like most Christians who experience trials and tribulations, I was asking, "God, why me? Why my family?" Everybody in the room was either crying or in a daze. When I was finally able to speak, I said to my mom, "My head is pounding." At that point, the headache and heartache combined scared me. I only said that to warn my family. I really felt that something was malfunctioning in my head. Something was happening. I was losing it. I was losing me. I accepted water and Ibuprofen from my mom. When I looked up to consume the water and medicine, I saw my dad sitting on the couch. He looked like a statue. His eyes were red. He was not crying, but I could tell he had been crying. He looked dead. My sister walked downstairs after unsuccessful attempts to find my inhaler. Her eyes were swollen and red. I could tell she, too, had been crying.

It was not about who was crying and who was not. I just desperately wanted some sign that indicated this was all a lie. A nightmare. But, I could not find one. Everyone looked devastated. The house contained an eerie, heavy spirit. There was no sign of Fabe, his skinny jeans, Ferragamo cologne, or mohawk with blonde tips. I did not hear him conversing loudly or laughing on the back porch. I did not know this type of pain, but I knew shortness of breath. I was experiencing a self-invoked anxiety attack. I had done it before. My head was pounding. My heart was bleeding. The tone of my mom's voice indicated that this night was going to get worse before it got better. I became disoriented and mad as hell! My mom's phone was ringing continuously. During one of the calls, she held the phone and listened more than she spoke. I assumed that someone was on the other end providing information. I asked the others in the room several questions but received very few answers. I learned that my brother had been shot at Coaches Bar and Grill in Atascocita. Fabe had mentioned Coaches several times. I knew that he visited that bar for games and drinks in the past. The fake friend in the room acted like he did not know where the bar was located, but I knew for sure that my brother had mentioned them going there together in the past. As the details started to unfold, it became even more difficult to regulate my thoughts and my breathing. I learned that my brother had already been dead for 7 hours by the time I found out. To say that "it goes down in the DM" is an understatement. My parents had already been to the murder scene. My mother mentioned seeing my brother's car in the parking lot of Coaches, roped off. She saw my brother from the left, still sitting in the car hours after he had been murdered. She said that there were several people at the scene; some claiming to be Fabe's friends.

Ugh! I felt this was all a curse, so I was cussing internally. Although no one else could hear me. God heard me. Besides, that's who I was mad at. Who else would I blame? I knew that He was all-knowing, and all-powerful. I felt that no matter what happened, God either arranged it or allowed it. My mom left my side to answer calls...mostly from family in Mississippi. I could hear her response, but I wondered what they were saying. I was dying to know more. I still did not know what happened, when, why, or who. My thoughts were racing!

I should not have gone to that damn prison today! My mama said I needed to rest anyway. I completed a 12-hour drive and slept for less than 12 hours over the course of 3 days. I love serving and volunteering with the ministry, but I should not have gone TODAY. For HOURS, I had ministered to them through song, words, and worship. Conscientious of the fact that the chapel was filled with different motives; not all were men after God's own heart. Most of them chose to talk more about victimization they had experienced than the offense they had committed. If you asked any one of them, they would have said their life was at its lowest. My brother was dead. Was there any point lower than that?

God spoke, again. *Wait a minute? So now you think death is punishment? O, yea of little faith. Don't you remember that for a believer, death is a reward?*
I had heard that all my life. I did not wanna hear that now. How could a reward hurt so badly? I'm sure the bullets hurt my brother. His death hurt me.

That night, there was an interview aired on the news with a guy named Dillon. He mentioned that He and Fabian were good friends and "grew up together." I became very suspicious because Fabian had not grown up in Houston. Also, what "good friend" has made time to complete a news interview but has not had time to contact your immediate family? Dillon was a young, Caucasian guy, and I did not know who that character was. I had never seen him before. He stated, "Maybe he got with the wrong crowd." His statements seemed rehearsed, superficial, and inconsistent with his allegation of them being "good friends."

It was getting late. The fake friend left first, and I told everyone how I felt about him. I suggested that my parents not allow him to return, especially until they received more information about what had happened to my brother. While we were talking, I heard the doorbell ring. My mother opened the door to find an officer. Our porch light illuminated his chocolate skin, badge, and weapon. I overheard him tell my mom that it was confirmed that my brother, Fabian Smith, was found murdered in the driver seat of his car. I guess he had not examined us as closely as I had examined him, because he acted like he was delivering an unknown message. It took the power of God to prevent me from replying, "Sir, do you have anything good to say?" Shortly after, our family friends left.

I looked over and was amazed at how my mother was the toughest of us all. But, she stated several times that it seemed unreal. I have always considered my faith to be the foundation on which I stand. God was my rock. But this shook up everything for me. Oh yeah, I was a saint with sinner problems. I searched for ways to serve God every day. He had moved mountains in my life. Fasting and praying were my remedies. I admit, sometimes I acted like I had no sense. But, Sundays were different. On Sunday, Lord knows I tried. I kept count of my sin on that day. I worked hard to keep that number as low as possible. I rarely wore dresses and preferred no makeup. I strived for decency and order. I was more generous than usual. I substituted cuss words for all kinds of silly stuff. I refrained from listening to rap music. I did not always agree with the rules that came with religion, which is why I chose a multidenominational church. But on Sunday, I found myself fighting to uphold the rules that had been instilled during my childhood; even the ones I did not agree with or really think would keep me out of the pearly gates of heaven. This one night was making me question all of that.

    The next day was a holiday – President's Day. My dad and my Uncle Tek arrived and provided much needed emotional support. Within hours, they had already started preliminary funeral arrangements, but I still wanted answers to my questions. Why was my brother murdered? On Tuesday, February 21st, my Auntie Tabatha arrived from Georgia; another great source of emotional support. That evening, I went to bible study, because I knew I needed it more than ever before. I needed to hear another word from the Lord because I did not like the last few statements He had spoken to me. I was desperate for an opportunity to worship Him and be amongst believers. During worship, I remember feeling limp as liquid from carrying such heavy pain. Within the first 48 hours of learning that my best friend was murdered, I was running to God and away from Him. I was so confused.

"Tragedy is usually a prolific teacher." – Pastor Keion Henderson

II. The Criminal (in)Justice System

Rampant injustices plagued the nation around the time of my brother's murder. I became petrified when the killer was apprehended because he did not look like me or my brother. Caucasian-American law enforcement officers and civilians had gotten away with killing African-Americans for decades; it has yet to come to an end. I had trouble sleeping, and I knew I could not sleep on this case.

On Sunday, February 26, 2017, my family and I returned to Houston after burying my big brother. Upon return, we noticed the family Schnauzer had become very ill. He vomited and slept a lot. And when he was awake, he constantly paced the floor. After a few days, I perceived that his behavior was synonymous with grieving and depression. On Monday, February 27, 2017, I was headed back to work. When I left work on Friday, February 17, 2017, I was enthusiastic about going home to see my new nephew. However, I was returning sick and sad. In addition, my commute was 51 miles which equated to one hour and 15-minutes in the car. As a result of my brother's horrific murder, I struggled with extreme levels of anxiety when I was alone in a vehicle. Although the murderer was apprehended a few days prior, I developed a new habit of constantly checking my mirrors for suspicious activity. I worried that someone may be following me and was planning to murder me too, in my car. In the midst of my paranoia, my phone rang and nearly caused me to wreck while driving westbound on Katy Freeway. On the other end of the phone, a family friend in Mississippi said, "Good morning, are you headed to court?" I was thinking, "Uh oh! Here we go!" I did not know what to expect. I asked her how she became aware of court. She stated that she had been following the case online since Tyler Green's arrest and learned that court was scheduled for 9 AM. I had not been

The Criminal (in)Justice System

informed prior to the phone call, so I thanked her for the information, but questioned the reliability of her statement. I could not afford to not know, so I made a U-turn, and proceeded towards the courthouse. I had been in and out of courtrooms for at least five years during my criminal justice career, but I knew this would be different. Fabian was not my client; he was my brother. For twelve months, I arranged my life around monthly court appearances. Court was exhausting! It usually consisted of me requesting off from work, paying $5-$20 for parking, cramming into slow elevators, and sitting for three to seven hours and observing the impacts of our broken criminal justice system. Harris County is a different type of beast. The TSA security checkpoints at the airport are comforting in comparison to entering Harris County's criminal courthouse.

My mom joined me for court in March 2017. During court, I could see her trying her best to stay strong. She looked extremely nervous. Her knees were locked, and she sat taller and straighter than the number 1. She asked me several questions from a small opening between the right side of her top and bottom lip. We were probably one question away from being kicked out because the rule was "no talking." Once I showed her Tyler Green, I could see her staring at him. I wondered what was going through her mind. The prosecutor spoke with us briefly afterwards, and my mom became very emotional. I looked away because seeing her cry made me feel pitiful as there was nothing I could do to ease her pain. I did not see any tissues anywhere, and I refused to leave her alone with the prosecutor while I went to the bathroom for tissues. He kept speaking in terms of the case and the cause number. I did not know if he realized that he was talking to a mother about her baby boy. A seven pound, 14.5-ounce baby she had given birth to at the age of 17. He was born with complications and died in an even more complicated way. Birthing him could have cost her life, so I feared that losing him could do the same. I wanted support. I needed support. But, I did not think my mom deserved to sit through this. So, I ended up at all other court appearances alone.

Court was typically scheduled for the first Tuesday of each month during "rocket docket." Initially, I had no idea what "rocket docket" meant. Nothing about these court dates was quick. Although court was scheduled to begin at 8 AM, the Judge did not usually start until 9 AM, and the word "start" was subjective. For every appearance, I had to request off a full day from work. There was no consistency. No one seemed to have any answers to my questions. Case files in manila folders were stacked in bins. The court room was often so packed that we had to sit closer together on the benches than we do on church pews.

Attorneys came in and out as they were often stretching themselves between more than one courtroom. The bailiffs scanned the room for reasons to remove an individual; there were others in the waiting area who would quickly fill the seat. Every month, there seemed to be more cases on the docket than the preceding month. While we waited and did not really know what we were waiting for, the court room actors ran circles around the room. I felt dizzy after watching them. I remember having pressing questions I attempted to obtain answers to throughout the month. I could not get any answers via phone or email. I would get to court and be within a few feet of the individuals I attempted to reach the other three weeks of the month, with no success. I thought about ways this hectic environment may have been used to 1) coerce innocent people into guilty pleas, 2) encourage judges to try cases with minimal information, and 3) discourage victims and advocates from taking part in this whole process. In addition to being hectic, this process was intimidating. I sat through hundreds of trials watching as attorneys appeared to be unprepared and unaware. Although I was not a defendant being represented by any of them, their shuffling papers and stuttering at the judge's bench made me nervous.

For this case, I was assigned a role that I had never assumed before: sibling of deceased victim. I found my interaction with Harris County Criminal Court personnel to be revictimizing at times. By the second appearance, I decided that I would start journaling to process what I was experiencing. Please see below for a few of my journal entries:

April 04, 2017 – Inside the criminal court building in one of the most dangerous cities in the United States. The court staff is engaging in casual, unrelated conversation. They're laughing, smiling, and joking. Some of us are scared to death. Well, I am. There are rapists and murderers in here, and the only protection I have is my notebook and pen. The elevators are always crowded. They're slow and they stink. I'm scared to breathe in or out; there's no telling what's in the air. I heard two men talking. One dressed in a two-piece suit, and another... well, let's just say he wasn't. I heard one of the men ask, "How did we get you out on bond? The other man replied, "PR." The first man said, "Man, I'm good." I thought, "Good for who? Who really benefits from your actions? Who suffers as a result of them?" I entered the courtroom and noticed that 80% of the staff appear to identify with the majority race while the offenders and others appear to identify with a minority race. Tyler Green's family had requested the $50,000 bond be lowered to $40,000. I left court enraged! On my way home, I thought long and hard about my response. I didn't know what to do, but I knew I had to do something. I wrote the following in my notepad: WE ARE RESPECTFULLY REQUESTING YOUR SUPPORT AS WE SEEK JUSTICE FOR FABIAN "FABE" SMITH. FABIAN WAS MURDERED IN THE PARKING LOT OF A STRIP CENTER AROUND 2 pm ON 02/19/2017. FABIAN WAS MURDERED BY TYLER GREEN, AN EX-

COWORKER, AND SOMEONE HE THOUGHT OF AS A "BUDDY." THE MURDERER, TYLER, INITIALLY HAD A BOND SET AT A MERE $50K. DESPITE AGGRAVATING CIRCUMSTANCES AND TYLER'S ALLEDGED PROBATION VIOLATION, HE AND HIS FAMILY ARE REQUESTING THE BOND AMOUNT BE LOWERED TO $40K. WE'RE BEGGING FOR YOUR SIGNATURE AND SUPPORT AS DECREASING TYLER'S BOND AND INCREASING HIS LIKELIHOOD OF RELEASE IS A DISSERVICE TO THE VICTIM, THE VICTIM'S FAMILY, AND OUR COMMUNITY. ON THE DAY OF THE OFFENSE, TYLER WAS CAUGHT ON SURVEILLANCE AT SEVERAL DIFFERENT LOCATIONS DRESSED IN A TOP HAT AND TRENCH COAT INCLUDING JUMPALOOZA (AN INDOOR PLAYGROUND FOR CHILDREN). WE ARE PLEADING THAT TYLER'S BOND NOT BE DECREASED AT THIS TIME. HELP US TO BE THE VOICE FOR THE VICTIM!

The judge reduced the murderer's bond before the offense report was received. She did not know the details of the case and neither did I. But, I knew that anyone who would murder an unarmed person around 2:00 PM on a Sunday, and had yet to give a reason, posed a threat to others. I knew I had to do something. I feared that injustice was brewing. I started a petition and quickly gained the support of over 1,000 members of the community. I was begging the judge to not lower the bond. I understood that bail was not designed specifically to hold a Defendant until trial unless certain criteria was met. But, I did not understand why so much courtesy for a killer? Why lower the bond and increase his opportunity to regain his freedom? This same level of courtesy had not been extended to the deceased victim. As a matter of fact, the request was made by the murderer's family, but I was told that the judge would not hear from me or anyone else from the victim's family during the pre-trial phase.

April 12, 2017 - My family in Mississippi has added flowers and other things to my brother's grave. My petition made the newspaper. Kim sent me a picture of the article. I knew that awareness was key; the community needed to know what I was experiencing. I was worried, I was scared, and I was distracted. I heard a voice say, "After you have taken the time to learn their language, they'll take the time to listen to you". I'm a fighter, but I understand that victory belongs to Jesus. I am worried that my boldness and the publicity may prevent me from securing other opportunities. I was too late. The bond has been lowered.

I did not know it then, but this was the onset of a perpetual cycle of winning and losing for me.

April 17, 2017 – That damn murderer has bonded out. I must make sure the protective order is in place for my family. God, you said you wouldn't put more on me than I can bear. I just wish I saw me the way that you see me. This all seems like way too much.

May 09, 2017 – My birthday is in 8 days. Who cares? The Prosecutor stated that the killer called my brother several times after he shot him. I guess to confirm that he was dead? How could he not be?

July 24, 2017 – The Prosecutor and I met after I had waited for three hours to speak with him. The Prosecutor stated, "This may have been a hate crime. There is speculation that he was racist. Several witnesses have come forward." This came as no surprise. The murderer was wearing black shades, a black top hat, and a black trench coat. On the surveillance video, he looks like a slave driver. Suddenly,

Murdered by a Christian, On a Sunday

I'm reminded of the "hat man legend" and the "top hat demon". Several weeks ago, a criminal attorney (who works with one of my mentors) gave me information for a civil attorney. She and I talked about how much this whole situation was costing my family. The criminal attorney said the civil attorney could help me, and that most families of murder victims hire a civil attorney pretty quickly. I called the civil attorney last week. He returned my call today and stated that there's nothing he can do to help me "unless the murderer has substantial resources." I have no idea. Am I supposed to know? With this, too, I'm trusting God. I hope Fabian is resting, because I sure am not. We laid him away well and took him back home to the coast to be near family and friends. But, now we're suffering and being revictimized by the criminal justice system. I have a four-year degree in this field. Five years of experience. I learned the processes and the system. So, I thought I had. I feel more lost than ever before. I expressed frustration with the lack of communication from the criminal court. The criminal attorney told me, "Attorneys have a way of making you disappear if they want you too." I replied, "That's exactly how I feel. I guess he's already done that." I wanted to tell her, "Well, aren't you encouraging?" That was the last thing I wanted to hear, although I knew that to be true. But, I am encouraged! If I give up, then my brother's life just disappears. I'm trusting God through this, too.

August 10, 2017 – This is not right! As a Community Supervision Officer, I had probationers charged with Theft and Aggravated Sexual Assault of a Child on my caseload. I knew that they all still had rights. There was certain information that they were privy to and I was required to provide within very specific time frames. I could not ignore calls or emails. I could not refuse case updates. The fact that I had more cases than I had been trained to handle could not be used as an excuse for ineffective case management. The unreal expectations could never justify my lack of compliance with professional standards. But with this case, I have not had much success with anyone up to this point. One of my mentors has been so patient with me. He's listened to me at times when I didn't even know what to say. After I told him all that I have experienced, he doesn't believe that Kim Ogg, District Attorney, is aware. I decided to draft a letter of my concerns to be forwarded to her.

My two greatest concerns (that can actually be resolved) are communication and resources.

1. Communication (and lack thereof)

I had no idea that, in trying to communicate with the court coordinator and prosecutor, I was opening the door to re-victimization. Please see below for just of few of my experiences:

- For my brother's murder case, **I received no notification that the offender had made bail**. When I contacted the prosecutor, I was referred to the victim services department. The representative explained how to register with vinelink, and I reiterated that **I was registered with VineLink**, but received nothing, so there was a possible glitch in the system. The offender was out on bail for at least two weeks before I was aware. (Updated 11/29/2017 - The offender bonded out again sometime during the month of November, and again I received no notification from VineLink.)
- My **case was assigned a new prosecutor, and no one contacted me**. I appeared in court and sat for over an hour, waiting to speak with TM. (Updated 11/29/2017 - On 11/21/2017, The prosecutor called and stated that he's being assigned to a new court. It is possible that this case will be assigned its 3rd prosecutor.).
- **The judge allowed and approved a request to decrease the bond amount from the offender's family**. When I mentioned to the prosecutor that the victim's family (and almost 1k members of the community, via a petition I started on change.org) was in opposition and concerned about the threat he posed to others, **the prosecutor replied**, "She's the Judge, she can do whatever she wants. This isn't the

part of the process where she'll hear from the victim's family." (the murderer was on probation when the murder was committed, violated probation and conditions of bond, and has been allowed to bond out again.)
- Since April 2017, **I've sent several emails and left voice messages for the court coordinator and lead clerk but received no response.**
- During one court appearance, the defense attorney called the offender to follow him out of the courtroom. Once they returned, the attorney stated, "have a seat right there." The **defense attorney motioned for the offender to sit next to me**. I was appalled.
- Recently, the prosecutor mentioned that the offender "didn't take the 40-year plea". I have no idea when this took place. I had no idea the prosecutor was even planning to offer a plea. He never discussed this with me or my family.
- During the August court appearance, after receiving no response from emails or voice messages, I walked up and asked the court coordinator, Kim Neely, if the offender was on the docket or if he had been reset. She replied "Who are you? You can't just be walking up here like that." I was never given the opportunity to reply. She was unprofessional in her tone and failed to even look up from her computer while speaking to me. (Updated 11/29/2017 - I appeared for the September and October court appearance to find out that court would be held in the jail. I've asked the prosecutor several times to communicate these things to me in advance.)
- My level of anxiety increased every time the prosecutor explained that he did not have the offense report and needed it by 05/23/17 "or," and he'd just end the sentence there. Even with an overwhelming amount of evidence, I'm still scared that the murderer could possibly get off on this charge because of these technicalities.
- The court personnel should be more mindful of how they communicate. We're more than paperwork; we're people. Although these examples are personal, they are real, and they depict a real issue with the communication and lack thereof. Despite having a Bachelor of Science in Criminal Justice and professional work experience in courts, corrections, and

community supervision, I still feel lost. I can't fathom not having this experience/education. When professionals become desensitized and complacent, that's a problem that affects more than just victims. When communicating with the court personnel, I feel like they fail to acknowledge that Fabian Smith may represent a cause number for them, but that's my brother.

2. Resources

Victims need reliable, relevant resources. There may very well be resources available in Harris county, but who, within the courts/criminal justice system, really serves as a "bridge" between the victims and the services?

- The current system places way too much responsibility on the victim/surviving family. While experiencing trauma, victims may not even be aware of what services they need, so a professional should intervene. **Victims need a list/database of reliable and relevant resources that can be easily accessed**.
- After receiving the victim services information from the prosecutor, it took over a week before we received a response. She never asked how we were, if there was anything she could do to help, or available services. She mentioned the crime victims' compensation application. No "services" were ever coordinated.
- My brother was murdered while sitting in his car. I was given less than 24 hours to pick up the car once it was released from the Homicide Division. There is blood splattered all over the car. My brother's personal items (including remnants of a sonic slush and a Lunchable; my brother liked them both) are also scattered throughout. I'm still searching for a place to have the car cleaned.

I knew that Kim Ogg was extremely busy. Even if she had skimmed my document and only read what was in bold, my message would have been conveyed. When I took the time to create it, I had to accept that she may not read it all. I had already made up mind that I would do all I could with all I had to overcome this.

August 18, 2018 – Several people sent me the link for Houston Chronicle's article today!! Yesterday, the murderer was re- arrested! According to the bond violation report, Green did not submit to a drug and alcohol test as required by the court on August 1st and tested positive for opiates on August 3rd. I disagreed with the decreased bond because of the threat that Tyler posed to the community. Now, his drug use has me wondering if he's also a threat to himself? Lord, justice must prevail!

September 12, 2017 –The criminal courts were flooded during Hurricane Harvey. I got all the way downtown, only to find out that court is being held inside the jail today. I hate this, because I already feel "out of the loop".

October 17, 2017- I'm working in Galveston. I heard a man's voice in the hotel lobby. He sounded just like the prosecutor. Is someone following me? Surely, no one is following me. Either way, I don't want to hear his voice.

November 21, 2017 – Today, I cleaned Fabe's grave. I got rid of everything that looked weathered or was broken. I placed Christmas décor all over the grave. This turned out to be a messy job, but it was worth every second. I was ironing and getting ready to shower when I received a call from the prosecutor.
Prosecutor: So, I may have told you, I'm being reassigned to another court.
Me: No sir, you didn't. (What the hell?? We could possibly get a 3rd prosecutor! Ughh!).
Prosecutor: Well, I have been. My goal is to keep Fabian's case because it's murder - one of my most severe. And, I feel like I have a bond with you and the family.

The Criminal (in)Justice System

Me: (Dude, I don't even know who to trust right now. To get case updates is like pulling teeth. Everything seems so reactive instead of proactive. You call that a bond?) Thank you, Sir. We'd appreciate that. (I was livid but trying to stay cool. I was trying to control my shaking. I was scared that being assigned a new prosecutor required more vulnerability.)

Prosecutor: Also, you may have known that Tyler did make that $120k bond a few days ago? Me: (What the hell! Really? Dude, why was he even still eligible for bond? Do you have any good news? Just ruin my damn day why don't you?) No sir, I didn't; maybe because I'm traveling. (Maybe because this is my first damn holiday season without my brother and I'm so busy pretending everything is okay!)

Prosecutor: Well, he has conditions and I'll be checking in with his P.O. as usual

Me: (This shit is sooo unfair. I'm shaking. I feel weak. I feel like I can't win. This is so unfair.) Okay, thank you sir. (I wanted the conversation to be over so bad, so I could break down alone. No scriptures came to mind; I wanted to tell the Prosecutor some cuss words that I had overheard in an alley in Mississippi).

After that call, I didn't speak for several hours. I was mad. I felt like nobody was helping. There were people who I was committed too, connected too, who had million-dollar influence, yet they turned the other cheek. The pain and anger could not be concealed. My mom told me, "Pray. Give it to God. Stop let'n it ruin you. You gon' keep let'n it do you like that?" I knew she was right. I got myself together… hours later. All I wanted was a bible, a pistol, and some red lipstick. At that moment, I was no longer scared. I wanted revenge. I remembered and posted, "Vengeance is mine thus saith the Lord" (Romans 12:19). I needed to encourage myself. I felt like my family did not understand what I was experiencing with court. But truth is, I was not the only one who felt defeated by such a sick system. Back home in Mississippi, a family friend's brother (the same family friend who notified me of my first court date on Monday February 27, 2017) was murdered about six months before Fabe was murdered. She called to tell me that the murderer in her brother's case (25-year-old, African-American male) was being held under a million-dollar bond, but she did not even have a tentative court date. I knew I needed to count my blessings. Had the city of Houston not been flooded during Hurricane Harvey, we would have had trial during that first week of November. The prosecutor provided a tentative trial date of February 5, 2018. Fabe and I had reasons why we, as singles, were not particularly fond of February. Now, I had different reasons.

"Sometimes, God will cause you gloom, so he can get the glory." – Pastor Keion Henderson

III.　Good Grief

    I still don't understand death and dying. Besides, that is not something I have ever done before. My great-grandmother died in 2007. That was difficult for me because she raised my mother, and I spent a great deal of my childhood under her care. When my brother was murdered, I had not experienced a close family death in several years. I was not allowed to attend my Aunt Peaches' funeral; she died of cancer in 2000. My family thought I was too young to attend her service; they did not allow any of the children to attend. My mom quit her full-time job to care for my great-grandmother and aunt until they transitioned. When my mom moved my aunt and my great-grandmother into our home, that meant Fabe and I had to share a room, again. For us, we were just back to the basics. We shared a room before ever having our own room, so the change was not as difficult as some people may think. In fact, this time it was much easier because we were older and away from home a lot more often. The bunk beds were gone, so we did not have to fight over who would get top or bottom. I can remember watching as my aunt and great-grandmother's health declined. My mom's job got harder, and my loved ones started to look less like the people I had known. In reflecting, I feel like God gave me signs and time to prepare for their homegoing celebrations. My family and I knew they were gone to a better place and would no longer be in pain. I lost several paternal family members, but even for them, their deaths marked the end of their health battles and suffering.

    But this was different, so my response was different. My expectations were different. Fabe said he would be right back, and I believed him. He left his game console on, the bed linen pulled back, and snacks all over his room. I think he believed he would return too. He was younger and did not have a major diagnosis. His death was unexpected. On

February 19, 2017, I knew I needed help. I knew this was not something I would be able to do on my own. My employer took better care of me than I deserved. I received a sympathy card from the CEO when I was expecting a letter of termination. They paid for me to attend grief counseling and excused every one of my absences. They also excused my inability to focus and meet the expectations of my position. After only two sessions, the grief counselor recommended I have a psychological evaluation (psych eval). I was confused by her recommendation. During those two sessions, I revealed some of my concerns, and her response made me feel as though my concerns were valid… and pretty typical. If they were, then why did I need a psych eval?

Warning: Handle me with care; I never received the psych eval!

Since then, I have had so many encounters with doctors. I was prescribed more medicine in four months than I consumed in over 25 years, including sleep aids and antidepressants. One day, I looked at the medications while complaining about the cost. For the first time, I read the side effects closely. One pill bottle read: Side effects may include constipation, aggression, and suicidal ideations. That did it for me! Considering the way my life was going, I pictured myself being that 1%. I was worried I would be that one patient on the toilet, wanting to fight someone, but also wanting to drink a cocktail of cleaning products. I started crying (which had become my response to almost everything) and called my sister. I was hysterical and described the doctor with words that are not found in the bible (and for the ones that are, I used them in a slightly different context). I tried to return the medication. Walgreens rejected that transaction. I'm glad they did not know the grief counselor, or they probably would have agreed with her regarding the psych eval. I never consumed the medication as instructed, but now I was refusing to take it "as needed." I did not want the side effects or to become a victim of the opioid crisis. I prayed and asked God to heal me and protect me. I told him I felt the enemy was attacking my mind, but I also needed him to protect me from me!

On March 18, 2017, almost exactly one month after the tragedy, I contacted my dad's friend (a barber) via Instagram. I felt like I was losing control of everything, but my hair was one of the few things I maintained control of. I scheduled an appointment for a haircut and told him I needed to get in that same day. He apologized for my family's loss and asked me what he could do for me. I told him I wanted my hair cut. I entered his shop with a blunt, collar-bone length bob. I had worn my hair in that style for a while and had grown to love the versatility. That's the only style the barber had ever seen me wear. He stalled and repeated my requests several times, as if he wanted to confirm that I knew what I was asking for. He even asked, "What is your dad gon' say?" I'm grown, I really had not thought about it. I told him it would be fine and that my mom was much more opinionated than my dad. Our debate lasted for about 20 minutes. I became agitated because I knew if he would have started cutting when I asked him to, we would be almost done. He kept asking if I was sure I wanted it cut. He was honest and told me he did not want to cut all my hair off. I replied, "I've already lost what matters to me. Just cut this hair. Do you want me to start for you?" Eventually, the barber cut my hair and shampooed it. I could tell I had stretched him far beyond his comfort zone. He turned me around to a body-sized mirror, and I HATED IT! But, I could not show it. I was not in the mood to hear, "I told you so" or anything similar. When I looked in the mirror, I was staring at my dad and a few of my uncles. They are handsome, but I had no desire to be handsome. I tried to appear content and said, "It'll be fine. I'm gonna fix it when I get home!" I could not wait to cry in the car like Red in one of the best movies of all times, "Friday." Most of my hair was about half an inch in length. It looked spikey like my Schnauzer when he gets a fresh trim, but the texture was much drier and brittle. This, too, confirmed how unhealthy I was at that point in my life. I moved from my favorite seat on the third row, left side of the church to the third to last row, right side of the church. I was still trying to adapt to the Megachurch. The last thing I wanted was to appear on the big screen baldheaded, nose running, and tears falling. Sometimes, I even sat near the Deacons because I thought I could blend in. I really did not want to be asked "How are you?" or "How have you been?" I did not want to lie in church or feel pressured to answer according to their expectations, but also because their responses had become repetitive. It was hard for me to believe what they were saying because I did not see it. After some services, I walked away thinking they were praying for me and I was praying for me, but God did not seem to be answering calls from anybody on my behalf. I continued to avoid going certain places, seeing certain people, and posting pictures of myself on social media for several weeks. I wanted to be comfortable with being uncomfortable. I knew that people could be cruel and some of the comments people post reinforce insecurities if we are not confident in who we are. Contrary to my beliefs, when I finally posted a picture, I received several compliments. Someone told me, "after a woman cuts her hair, she grows with it." I had already planned that had the responses been different, I would use humor to get through it. I was prepared to tell anyone who asked that I had a Brittany Spears moment! As if I did not have enough to worry about, it was hard for me to look in the mirror because I knew my brother would not have agreed with my decision.

  In May 2017, despite that being my birthday month, I noticed my mental and physical health continued to decline. While I had gotten used to not sleeping, my mother and a friend recognized that I was not eating. It was not on my to-do list. If asked to name three things I had eaten over a three-day period, I would have struggled. When I was around family, I ordered food or fixed a plate to avoid attention. I would provide various reasons for not eating and discard the food as soon as I could.

I was not able to separate the stress and trauma. I have had asthma and bronchitis all my adult life, but I have experienced so many more triggers. On several occasions, my asthma decided to spend time with my anxiety. I would go from thoughts about my brother and crying, to shortness of breath and shaking. I developed a skin condition that was induced by stress. To avoid stares and stigma, I have spent the past year of my life covering most of my arms, back, and chest. This has been extremely difficult. I'm a southern girl. Wherever I am, it is usually HOT! I am forced to wear sleeves no matter the temperature, and scarves have become my favorite accessory. A hot bath would have provided some time for me to relax and engage in self-care, but I was instructed to limit my shower to lukewarm water for about seven minutes and to avoid baths altogether. My nail biting worsened, especially when I engaged in deep thought. I bit my nails and cuticles until they became painful. I was so embarrassed. I was already withdrawing from others because the stress had caused physical changes (weight loss, but more recently weight gain). I also avoided any interaction that would require me to shake hands or do anything that would bring attention to my fingers. In the past, manicures and nail polish were deterrents. In this season, my nerves were so shot that I bit the polish off too. I became so confused that I could not retain much of anything. Not even the word of God. I can remember not being able to sleep and opening my bible, begging God to comfort me. I would attempt to read any scripture that caught my eye. I thought I was losing my mind because I could not comprehend words that had been instilled in my mind and heart as far back as I could remember.

In September 2017, for the first time in nine months, I slept with the light off. Up until then, I had slept with the light on or not slept at all. Even now, that is a decision I usually make after I shower. Every day is different, but now I have a smaller lamp that fills the void I once used my room light to fill. I avoid total darkness as it seems to facilitate my fears. I understand God did not give me a spirit of fear, and I will never argue that he did. When I needed that light on, I was dealing with the consequences of my doubt. When I started questioning God, the decrease in my faith resulted in an increase in my fears.

I knew I had to persevere, but I doubted whether I could. Over a 12-month period, I questioned my core, my foundation, and my God. I thought He was punishing me. I thought He had taken my brother to settle an account for sins I had committed. I forgot all about the incidents on Calvary. The pain was so deep I thought I would die. In all honesty, I wanted to die, and I did not need any medication for assistance. The main reason I did not organize and execute a plan was because of my mom. My mom had just buried her baby boy, and I did not want her to have to bury me. The thoughts of no longer wanting to live seemed so selfish. I went from being a healthy, driven, young woman to a very sick, confused, and confrontational skeleton. I fought. I fought with my family. I fought the trauma. I fought with God, and I am so thankful that I lost! I was mad at God, because I thought He was mad at me. I went from attending worship service every Sunday and Tuesday (and any service in between) to sometimes once a month. I became an e-member and streamed church from the discomfort of my home. I knew all along it was not equivalent to attending church. I never regarded it as the same. I was used to fighting and maintaining my distance from whoever I fought with, but I could not get away from God. Now, I know what my great-grandmama meant when she said, "He kept me when I didn't wanna be kept." I attended school about 14 hours each week and my classes were located inside a church. I did not know this until after the semester began. I agreed to help a friend out with his business which was also located inside a church. I did not know this until I called him to confirm what the right turn my GPS instructed me to take. I was there at least 24 hours each week. Although I was questioning God's love for me and his plan for my life, He provided opportunities that required me to be in his house more than my own house. I was surrounded by his Word. Even when it did not make sense, He forced me to see it.

My questioning elevated from "why is this happening to me" to "why am I responding in this way?" I noticed my threads on social media looked like the obituary section of the Sun Herald, so other people were experiencing death as well. But because of the mental health stigma within the African-American community, I was not comfortable sharing my deepest, darkest moments with anyone. I felt that even if they could relate, they would not say so. In comparison to other cultures I had developed relationships with, my people were less likely to have access to mental health resources, less likely to utilize the resources, and less likely to support our family and friends who needed the resources. Some of my thoughts and behaviors were so far from who I knew myself to be (and from who I wanted to be) that I became angry. I was starting to get on my own nerves. I previously mentioned I did not like being in my car, or any car, alone. In addition to checking the mirrors to confirm no one was following me, I had to keep the rear seats and floor clear of large items to make sure no one was hiding inside the car. One day, I was cleaning my rear seats and found papers underneath my laptop bag. They were papers from the grief counselor. My sessions had ended, and I had not been to visit her in months. The papers included the referral for a psychological evaluation and several other pages. One page included the words anger, denial, and depression, so I knew I needed to review the document more carefully. I had experienced all three that day. It was an explanation of the stages of grieving. I could not make sense of anything that was happening in my life, but suddenly, my reactions did not seem as bizarre. So, maybe the grief counselor's knowledge of this cycle is why she acted like my concerns were expected. But, that lead me back to one of my original questions: why did I need a psych eval? The document includes a timeline from the week of the loss up to two years following the lost. I have included a snippet of this document (Appendix A) for review only.

If you have experienced a loss and any of the thoughts or feelings listed, please seek professional help. If you are considering hurting yourself or someone else, please contact 911 or the National Suicide Prevention Lifeline (1-800-273-8255) immediately.

During my highs and lows, I continued writing in my journal – the same journal I was using to process my experiences with court. At the time, I did not know some incidents impacted me the way they did, but now I know these incidents interfered with my grieving process and served as triggers.

July 18, 2017 – My mom told me she was at a sports bar near her home, wearing her necklace that has my brother's picture on it. The Waiter (my mom described her as a young, Caucasian girl) seemed surprised at the sight of my mom's necklace. She told my mom, "I knew Tyler. He was a monster. I knew Fabian. He was my friend." The Waiter apologized for my mom's loss, became emotional, and walked off. When my mom shared this story, I wondered, "Why didn't somebody stop him before he got to my brother?"

August 28, 2017 – I am so scared. The semester just started, and here comes Hurricane Harvey. Family and friends are calling. Here I go again, pretending to be okay. I evacuated to Dallas, alone. I feel so guilty for leaving my family in Houston, but what was I supposed to do? I can't really afford to lose anything else. As a matter of fact, I can't even afford the insurance deductibles. My income is already less than half of what it was before Fabe was killed because it's extremely hard for me to work anything close to 40 hours each week. I chose to get water, gas, and non-perishable food items while my family chose to decorate for a Mayweather Fight Party. My aunt is near, and I'll stay with her until I wear out my welcome. Her house is big, so hopefully she won't notice me sleeping with the light on. Oh! She has a bathroom right next to the guest room. I'll leave that light on; that doesn't seem abnormal. When she's at work, I don't know what I'll do. All my friends in the Dallas/Ft. Worth area are really Fabe's friends. I haven't seen or talked to some of these people since he was killed. I really wish he was here with me. If FEMA provides a hotel room or recommends I go to a shelter, I don't want to go by myself. As tough as this is, it's tougher because I'm alone. My great-grandmama is calling and telling me to come home. I would if I could.

October 17, 2017- I saw Fabe spinning in a computer chair in the game room. It was about 2:00 AM, but I wasn't scared. That's about the time he and I really acted silly. I just waited patiently for what was next. He didn't say anything. I guess he just stopped by to check on me. I had been up for several nights unable to sleep. He and I used to go to Walmart during late nights and early mornings. He liked to freestyle and dance up and down the aisles. He would do almost anything to entertain me and the Walmart stockers.

Murdered by a Christian, On a Sunday

October 18, 2017 – I don't know what happened last night, but I really miss my brother. I want him back!!

November 2, 2017 - I'm so happy my mom wants to get rid of Fabe's car too! I had a conversation with my dad already about how hard it is for me to pull in the driveway and see that car there but accept that Fabe is not home. We covered the bloody seat with a blue tarp, but at night the tarp looks like a body bag and it's in the driver seat, so I imagine it's my brother. That car also had to have costly repairs just days before he was killed. It is the reason he didn't go home with me to see our nephew. I don't ever want to see that car again!

November 19, 2017 - Nine months ago to the day, my brother was murdered. 9 months. The length of a full-term pregnancy. Biblical scholars may refer to 9 as the number of finality or judgment. A perfect movement of God. It's the number of patience. I feel so confused right now. I have more problems than I have solutions. I'm tired of me and them. I miss my brother. I'm an introvert at my core; I don't really want to go anywhere, but I want to be invited. Lord, I'm struggling, and I know it is a result of me taking my eyes off you. I haven't been to church or bible study. I feel like I'm filled with so much hell right now. Lord, deliver me. I'm grieving. I have less control than ever before, but I want more control. I'm lonely. I'm broke. It's Thanksgiving, and I need to be more thankful. I feel so bipolar. Lord, help me get my mind right. I pray tomorrow will be different. I'll do everything I can to make it so. Lord, protect me from the fakes. To all the people I've hurt, please let them know that I am sorry. This week alone, I have had more fights, arguments, and cussed more than I can stand. I know it's an attack of the enemy. A distraction. Lord, deliver me from myself. This is the year of elevation. Lord, I know you won't take me up if I keep acting low.

December 31, 2017 – I'm in Virginia enjoying the holiday break with an old friend. It's nice to catch up because he has his own memories with my brother. He remembers that growing up, my brother and I were a package deal. He was a friend to us both. We laughed as I fought to hold back the tears. He has his own issues, so I won't burden him with mine.

January 5, 2018 – I have been planning my brother's 30th birthday party for over a month now. Today, the planning doesn't seem as exciting. It seems unfair. Two people have told me they did this for a deceased family member and will never do it again. I wish I would have heard their statements sooner. This is confusing and exhausting. Need I mention my Uncle Reb died yesterday? He took me shopping for school supplies for several consecutive years during grade school. I didn't know why he was taking my siblings and I to buy new supplies while other kids were getting new shoes and clothing. It all makes sense now. He was setting us up for success. I kinda feel numb to death and I don't like this feeling. I did not shed a tear for my uncle but hearing my grandmother's voice was painful. I sent her flowers today. She supported me when I lost my brother. She just lost her last one. I need to be there for her.

January 6, 2018 – My emotions are out of control. Lord, I need you to help me control them. I'm doubting what I see and what I don't see. I don't want to end up in a padded room.

March 6, 2018 - My 5-year-old cousin and I were headed to bible study. She absolutely loves bible study and church! She loves to worship. I told her tonight was the Black History

Month Program. She asked me about the different things that would take place.
Her: Do they have a picture of the devil there?
Me: No baby, we worship God.
Her: What does the devil look like?
Me: Evil and ugly with red horns on his head I think.
Her: I know what the devil looks like.
Me: What?
Her: Like that boy that killed Fabe.
Me: You're right, that is what the devil looks like.
Afterwards, I wondered if I should have explained Ephesians 6:12, "For we wrestle not against flesh and blood, but against principalities, against powers, against the rulers of the darkness of this work, against spiritual wickedness in high places." Because I'm constantly praying for increased understanding, I didn't know how to articulate that conversation to a 5-year-old. There is no telling what she's heard us talk about. Ugh, this could result in secondary trauma for her. Lord, help today!

March 10, 2018 – I'm at Starbucks because I have trouble focusing to complete anything at home. I keep hearing them refer to one of the Baristas as "Tyler". That name disgusts me. Ugh. He is also a young, Caucasian male. The name alone doesn't sound threatening at all, unless your brother was murdered by a Tyler. It's not fair that it doesn't carry the same stereotypes as DeAndre, Trevon, or Jamal. I'm glad my mom named my brother Fabian. That one is a little less common for an African-American male. Here in Texas, I've met a few Hispanic males named Fabian. Well, they are also subjected to bias and prejudice.

"And we know that in all things God works for the good of those who love him, who have been called according to his purpose." (Romans 8:2

IV. Is This What You Called Me For?

During the Fall semester of 2016, I was enrolled at Sam Houston State University (SHSU) as a Graduate Student. I was that student whose one semester break after earning my undergraduate degree resulted in four years of being an adult. Every year, I had more excuses, better excuses, which prevented me from furthering my education. I lied to myself year after year. Some people refer to that as procrastination. Considering the salary for my first job after college as a state employee, I knew something had to change. Before tax, I was middle class. After tax, I touched the poverty line. As a matter of fact, I worked at least two jobs for 10 years. Now, when people ask, "What do you do?" I respond, "Whatever is required." They usually get offended and think I'm trying to be smart. I am. Because what I did for so long was not.

I completed my undergraduate degree at SHSU and was excited about returning. I was majoring in Victimology/Victim Studies. After about five years of working with offenders in corrections, courts, and community supervision, I was hungry for the other side. I had interacted with victims during homes visits and incoming calls as a Community Supervision Officer, but my schedule had not permitted me to gain much insight into their perspective. I was three months into the Graduate program, and I loved it! My professors were amazing, and I consumed a wealth of new information. I thought about family members who had been victimized. I remembered stories I had been told by offenders. As an Intake Officer in corrections, some of my fellow officers would argue that the offenders were "playing the victim." I understood what they meant and how important it was for offenders to accept responsibility on the road to rehabilitation. But, so much of my course material discussed the cycle of victimization.

Most of us have heard, "hurt people, hurt people." I believe that statement, without minimizing actions or shifting blame. As with any offense, there are aggravating and mitigating circumstances. I think having experienced victimization falls somewhere in between the two.

Because the graduate program was half the length of the undergraduate program, I was only 3 months in and thinking long and hard about what I wanted to do upon graduation. I knew I did not particularly care to return to a state agency. I was not aware of any agencies in my area that offered victim services in the way I envisioned them. My search yielded state and local agencies and a few non-profits. Their mission statements were filled with action words, but so was the mission statement for the Texas Department of Criminal Justice. I went from searching to worrying in a matter of days. I contacted family members who work in other sectors and live in other geographical locations, specifically more liberal states. I was privileged to speak with a retired judge, professor, and an activist in California. I asked her more about her work and interests. I also told her my major and described the program. She responded, "What are you gonna do with that?" I appreciated the feedback, but as the conversation persisted, I started to question whether the program was preparing me for my long-term goals.

The semester was ending, and the holidays were approaching. I knew if I blinked during the holiday dinner, we would be in a new year. I did not want to start a new year with old concerns. I decided to research a little more. I began to think about what the agencies offered and what I planned to offer. I surfed agency websites, their services and their salaries. The results were discouraging. For the agencies that were closest to the city's center, the salaries would not cover living expenses for housing within a 10-mile radius. Because of my previous experiences and career choice, I did not give it much more thought. I decided I would not return to school for the Spring semester. I never prayed about it. It was one of the many decisions I made without consulting God, because I was not really ready for His response. I knew there was a chance that my wants did not align with His will. All on my own, I decided to take another break to "get myself together." I figured to major in Victimology/Victim Studies must have been the result of poor decision making and that I needed to think longer and harder about what I really wanted to do. It seemed irrational to earn a master's degree in an area where my annual return would be less than my initial investment. Had I chosen to give Sallie Mae every check I earned for 12 months, that would not repay the student loan. Nah. I wasn't doing it.

    The semester ended. I had earned all As and one B. I had developed a professional relationship with one of my professors and managed to get a letter of recommendation from her after just four months. She was the only professor who I informed that I would not be returning for the Spring semester. She wished me well. Her email was so thoughtful and well-written that I felt undeserving. I felt it should have been for someone who had a plan. I did not know what I was quitting to do! During the holiday break, I informed my parents that I would not be returning to SHSU. They treated me like an adult, but I am not sure if that is what I needed at that time. They pretty much said, "If you choose to continue, we support you. If you choose to quit, just know that we support you." But not "support" as in pay for it. Which, in their defense, is probably why they provided little feedback. Ultimately, it was my life, my decision, and my expense, and they made that clear. I kept my textbooks! I spent the rest of the winter break thinking about what I would do with the next year and my life. I had this love/hate relationship with school. I have always loved to learn. I love school supplies, planners, and colored pens. I love lunch kits and backpacks. I like sharing what I have learned with others. But, I hated the cost of higher education. Mostly because I had not created a way to afford it without student loans. But, I also hated when others (like employers) did not value the cost or quality of higher education.

During the remainder of the holiday break, and the beginning of the new year, I engaged in independent study and embraced opportunities to attend conferences and seminars. I was (and am) drawn to anything about victims and their experiences. I was intrigued by research that explored incidents of victimization for offenders, especially while incarcerated. I continued to feed that hunger while working my full-time job, but without the cost of tuition. Well, 2017 was a roller coaster of a year, but that ride was over. Nevertheless, I was still experiencing its side effects.

In January 2018, I decided to deep clean and stumbled upon a church program that was 10 years old. It was the church program that was distributed at the service coordinated for all graduating High School seniors in the congregation. A section of the program included my plans after graduation. As I read the section, I remembered exactly where the information had come from. Me! I was given a questionnaire to complete. During my senior year in high school, I told my family, friends, and the church I planned to work with victims of crime. The passage was so elaborate. How had I let that go? How had I lost sight of that? How had I allowed my passion to be interrupted by the concern of no profit? That did not sit well with me. I knew the passage was almost copied and pasted from the questionnaire I completed. I have mentioned I was born into poverty. I have had countless number of broke days. I feared returning to the place where I started. But, I knew several people who were wealthy, but miserable. I knew the only way I would have my cake and eat it too was to operate within my calling. Whatever it was. Lord, is this what you called me to do? I asked him, but in all honesty, I still was not ready for him to answer. I had not really surrendered and given him control of that area of my life. I had bailed on God's people and a need that I was equipped to meet. I sincerely feel as though

God placed me in a position to need the services He had created me to provide for others. It helped me to understand the value of my gifts. I became so much more sensitive to the pain of others and the signs I was given. My perception of everything I experienced shifted. I had not experienced doubt and confusion merely because I had lost my brother. The greater issue was I did not know why I was created. I did not know what God had called me to do in such a massive city or on Earth. Although this is not the end of the story, it could be.

"Occupation is what you know how to do. Vocation is what God called you to do." -Pastor Keion Henderson

V. #FABE

It is probably pretty obvious that my life was all over the place. Not to imply that I have it all together now. I definitely do not. I was doing so much, but I felt like I could do more. The support I received from the petition I started on Change.org was somewhat unexpected. Comments from members of the community validated my concerns regarding injustice, gun violence, and the continued need for bail reform in Harris County. I knew I wanted to be a change agent, but I accepted the reality that I could not make significant changes alone.

I decided to incite a movement. I knew this tragedy needed some exposure. Based on the messages and calls I received, it was evident that my brother had not died in vain. I needed to connect with others, especially people with significant influence. More so, I needed the help of people who did not look like me, but understood that they, too, were impacted by injustice, rampant gun violence, and the corrupt bail system. I understood that privilege was a gentleman who only opened doors for some. I took inventory of my available resources. I did not have much, but I decided to use everything I had; including my mouth that had gotten me into trouble as a child. I was always inquisitive. I never struggled with speaking. I remember my dad took my siblings and I to an amusement park. When we reached the entry gate, I was clinging to my dad's leg, excited, but not knowing what to expect. The attendant asked, "How old is she?" My dad replied, "Four." I had to help him; my poor Dad was confused! I am the eldest daughter, but my dad was probably confusing me with my sister. I shouted to the attendant, "No ma'am, I'm si...!" My dad's hand covered my mouth like a major league glove, so I let him keep the "x". I knew if I wanted to continue through the gate, I would have to be four years old for a few more minutes. I was hoping there would be no consequences for my attempt to assist. Surprisingly, my dad has only spanked my sister and I once, but this was not that one time.

I decided that although I was an amateur to social media, I would establish a platform and use it to gain support for justice. I went through my very limited list of friends and quickly noticed that most of them looked like me and had little to no influence beyond social media. Up to that point, I was not a fan of Facebook. I saw how it had interrupted people's lives. I saw couples post their highs and lows, teens were running from the app because it was infested with adults, and employers were prioritizing Facebook searches over background checks. I spent a little time educating myself on the benefits of Facebook and was convinced it could increase my effectiveness and efficiency. I only had two thumbs. Venturing into twitter and snapchat would likely result in symptoms of Carpal Tunnel Syndrome, and I was not willing to take that risk.

Before eliciting support, I evaluated my mission and tried my best to assure my expectations were realistic. I identified small goals and larger goals. The smaller goals were mostly for me; goals that were measurable and quickly attainable, so I would maintain my momentum in the fight. I knew I would face disappointment. Besides, the movement was birthed out of disappointment. My larger goals were much more difficult to identify. Some were so large that I knew they may not be attained during my lifetime. I struggled with narrowing my focus. I was fighting injustices, grieving with limited resources, constantly anxious about my family's safety, and trying to figure out how to save someone else's brother. I was working to accept that I could not bring mine back. Despite all the negative I was facing, I needed to take a strengths-based approach to every issue in my life. Otherwise, I would be in the cemetery plot next to my brother.

#FABE

The movement is not about me, and I have always wanted that to be clear. God gave me the acronym FABE, which is also my brother's nickname, Forget Average Be Extraordinary. My brother was truly EXTRAORDINARY! He enjoyed socializing, fashion, music, and night life. His sense of humor could invoke a headache and a stomach ache at once. Growing up, he managed to make jokes out of things that would have made others fold. One time, Fabe purchased a car which did not have A/C or heating. He purchased a clip-on fan like the ones often found at the nail shop. The little white fans. He clipped the fan to the driver side visor. The fan was powered by rechargeable batteries, so Fabe allowed the fan to blow nonstop. I have a picture of him on one of Houston's hottest days, posing in the driver seat of his car with that fan blowing. I laugh because I can only imagine the hot air the fan must have been blowing! To this day, I believe Fabe had ADHD, but never received a diagnosis. I had never seen him tend to any one activity for more than a few moments. He became bored easily and preferred to stay busy. He was a salesman! He had worked several retail positions and was influential enough to sell you something you already owned or never considered buying. One day, I was on the phone, and he decided to market products during my call.

Fabe: Who is that?
Me: Kim
Fabe: Tell her I said Hey! Ask her if she wants to buy some whitening strips!
Me: That's kinda rude. I don't really want to her to think I'm implying anything. (It was too late; she heard him).
Kim: What did he say? (She laughed, so I knew she heard him. Maybe she just wanted to confirm what she heard.)
Me: Girl, that's my brother. (I was not repeating that! A few weeks prior, she had mentioned dental work, and I did not want her to think I discussed that with my brother.)

Murdered by a Christian, On a Sunday

Fabe: What did she say? I got some for her and her husband! (I tried to conceal my laughter, but I couldn't. He and I laughed so hard.)

He was so extra! He took pride in his smile and used whitening strips several times each week. His outfit had to color coordinate and his hair had to be neat. He visited his barber every Friday. After he was murdered, the owner of a local nightclub sent condolences via Facebook. Coincidentally, Fabe had lost his phone, and the owner found it. The owner returned the phone to me. He said whenever Fabe was in the club, he really enjoyed himself. He added that Fabe wanted to make sure everyone around him enjoyed themselves as well.

Although it was not about me, so many aspects of the #FABE movement were speaking to me. I loved to inspire people who were in challenging situations and on the verge of giving up. I know the cliché, but in this case, I had to preach it before I understood how to practice it. Because I truly believed that all things worked together for my good, I wanted to respond to this tragedy in an extraordinary way. I wanted to honor my brother's life in an extraordinary way. This tragedy altered my "ordinary" life, and I knew I would never be able to return to my normal. This was a great opportunity for me to define what extraordinary meant to me! I hired two different designers for a logo, assistance with branding, and clothing. I am forever indebted to them. They were patient with me and read my mind when I could not speak. Both provided flexible payments when my dreams exceeded my finances. Together, we designed a few different logos, shirts, and hoodies. The movement spread like a wild fire! Within a few weeks, I had shipped a hoodie to every southern state, the east, and west coast. Fabe supporters ranged from our 67-year-old grandmother to an 11-year-old who saw the movement on Instagram and wanted a shirt to show her support. It was mind-blowing!

Although I was in no rush to explore Snapchat or Twitter, our supporters took the movement to those apps. We used the following hashtags: #FABE #ForgetAvgBXtraordinary #RIHFabe #RIPFabe and #PowerofPeace. I am reiterating: I had no idea what I was doing. I embraced every day as an opportunity to learn and inspire others. Also, as a day to honor my brother. FABE was 29 years old when he was murdered. Very early on, I became personally committed to allowing him to live through me. However, the movement allowed me to connect with some individuals who were more extraordinary than I may ever be, so I challenged them to do the same. I shared that at the age of 29, FABE left with so many unfulfilled dreams and goals. I encouraged my supporters to go after their dreams, and together, we would see my brother's dreams come to fruition. The excitement and honor were contagious! Supporters were posting pictures, comments, and quotes using the hashtags. This was not my movement, this was our movement, and they respected it as such. Some of my favorite supporters include:

- A teacher wore her FABE gear to work and shared his story with her students
- A hairstylist wrote an amazing post supporting our advocacy efforts
- Several military personnel
- Family and friends would travel and post pictures with their FABE gear as a symbol that FABE was with them.

It got better with time! FABE was spotted enjoying a night on Bourbon Street in New Orleans, relaxing on a Caribbean cruise, and ziplining in Costa Rica.

Several supporters took FABE to see movies, (Black Panther was my favorite!) professional games, and concerts. My heart was filled with appreciation. For some of the most faithful supporters, I shipped some of Fabe's personal items (clothing, hats, cologne, deodorant, etc....). He meant so much to so many people, and I wanted them to know that I did not underestimate their relationships just because I am his sister. I continued to cry day in and day out. I must say, the support FABE received made me reevaluate my own life. I loved Fabe with everything in me, but I did not understand how he had touched so many OTHER lives in such a short amount of time. I knew that as hard as I had worked, as goal oriented as I had been, I could not compare to the person he had been to others. My resume was impressive, but I knew that had I dropped dead that second, my eulogy may not have been as impressive. I could never fill his shoes, and I would not try. But, I knew I needed to make some changes.

    I am an introvert at my core, and the murder of my best friend was forcing me to connect with others... understand and appreciate the opportunity to connect with others. Ugh, I had so much work to do! I started with just keeping it real. From the day my brother was murdered, and I told my mom I was okay to drive myself home, I had engaged in so much pretending. Especially if I thought it would protect her. I decided to be transparent about how I was responding to this whole tragedy. I prayed that my transparency would expedite healing. I posted when I was laughing about old memories or decided to raid my brother's closet and wear his clothing. I also posted when I was up at 4:00 AM crying and could not sleep. I posted significant anniversaries, but sometimes I posted because it was Sunday or the 19th day of the month. Nobody can dictate how I grieve; not even the cycles and charts which have helped me along the way. I thought about how Kanye West's life seemed to spiral after the death of his mother. When others had gone on with their lives and lost the bookmarks the funeral home provided, I was tangled up in those cycles. For some of my favorite Instagram and Facebook accounts, their fame is based on them posting the highlights of their life. I have had ups and downs, and I have strived to depict that

truth in my posts. This has not been easy. I encourage you to follow me on
Instagram: @findingfabe and Facebook: @Bee Smith. I pray it inspires you to get going on the work you were called to do!

Forget Average, Be Extraordinary
Statistics R "their" story; create UR own!
Empowering thru Transparency
Movement dedicated to Fabian "Fabe" Smith

This was only the beginning. Also inspired by my brother's death and what appeared to be an increase in mothers burying their babies, my mom used her Facebook page to launch "Sunday Son's Day." Every Sunday, my mom posts inspirational photos and quotes that depict her journey. The cycle of life was interrupted the moment the Homicide Detective confirmed her baby's body was found in the passenger seat of his car. Her grieving process looks different from mine, and I try to remain sensitive to that. I allow her to own that. Other mothers who have had similar experiences are able to relate on a level I may never understand. Her posts are consistently uplifting and in alignment with the FABE movement. She is also transparent.

She does not pretend to be okay on her difficult days. She shares moments of sadness, doubt, and regret. She continues to post pictures of her and FABE. Although he is no longer physically here, she has committed her life to being his Mom forever. Hence, her Instagram name: @mrsbambeefabiansmom. He was her oldest child, but he will always be her baby boy. I love the courage that shines through her vulnerability. She does not allow the circumstances to determine how she should live her life. She acknowledges that this will always be difficult, but not unbearable. Her life is forever changed, but she reminds us all that if she can do it, so can others.

Our hard work has not gone unnoticed. Because of the overwhelming support, my brother is now Google-able. Go google him right now! In February 2018, I was invited as the keynote speaker for a Black History Month Program in East Texas. A teacher recommended me as the speaker after seeing my advocacy work on social media. In April 2018, I was interviewed by a journalism student at the University of Houston. She stated that she had stumbled upon my brother's case and my advocacy work on Facebook. I was amazed that she would care enough about my brother's story to learn more and use his case for a semester long project. Here are some other examples of EXTRAORDINARY support we have received for my brother's life:

- Two additions to the family have been named Fabian
- Several friends and family have gotten tattoos of his name or face
- To acknowledge significant anniversaries related to his death, friends and family have gathered for several balloon releases
- Several independent artists have mentioned him in their songs

Although the petition has been declared a "victory," I encourage you to check it out at change.org[2]

Another one of my goals is to relaunch FABE as a nonprofit organization passionate about mentoring adolescent males. While privatized prisons are seeing an influx in investors, I am much more interested in disrupting the school-to-prison pipeline. My brother is gone, but I'm here to save someone else's.

FABE

---

[2] https://www.change.org/p/248th-district-court-justice-for-fabian-fabe-smith?recruiter=14016736&utm_source=share_petition&utm_medium=copylink&utm_campaign=share_petition.

Murdered by a Christian, On a Sunday

"Forget Average, Be Extraordinary"

(Use this page to define what EXTRAORDINARY means to you, and then go DO IT!)

-Bianca Smith

VI.   Trial

    I had never attended a murder trial. One of my younger sisters and my maternal grandmother loves to watch Law and Order, but I have never been a fan. As a matter of fact, I do not even like the audio. I have walked in on them watching the show and became uncomfortable with the sound effects and the voices of the lead actors. It never seems to start or end well. Although the show itself is fiction, I have always been concerned with not knowing which elements of the show are based on non-fiction. Most of the work I completed with felony cases was in Montgomery County, Texas. For narrative purposes, think of Montgomery County as Rhode Island and Harris County as Texas. I did not know what to expect, and that's when the worrying resumed. My faith was being tried…again!

    I conducted research on the proceedings of a murder trial, strengths and limitations within Harris County, and additional avenues I could use to advocate for justice. When I walked in on my sister watching Law and Order, I was intentional about leaving the room a little slower than I had in the past. However, I was cautious of my response to Law and Order for several reasons. The most obvious reason: because it is television. And the not so obvious reason: I was unable to catch one episode of Law and Order that depicted the story of an African-American victim. Even more surprisingly, very few of their stories depicted a male victim or an African-American offender. I was glad I tuned in! I could argue racial and gender bias, but I was relieved that the producers of Law and Order did not adhere to the same stereotypes as other shows.

    It all felt like a rollercoaster ride. I went from a period of little communication from the courts to unreliable communication. The details regarding trial changed so often; it was almost impossible to prepare. I was aggravated with things happening that were beyond my control. I simply told my professors and supervisors trial was approaching. I was unable to provide an exact date for quite some time. I had already missed so many days that I could have been academically dismissed from the graduate program and terminated from my job.

I journaled my way through this difficult process....

November 7, 2017 – I received a phone call regarding the trial date. I was told January 29, 2018, but I was also told it couldn't be confirmed at this time. This is so frustrating. When will they be able to confirm? My advocacy efforts have resulted in the case getting more exposure than other cases in Harris County. Maybe they're trying to avoid a mass turnout or support that may be deemed distracting during trial. My spiritual father said this is the year of elevation. This is the year God takes me higher in every aspect of my life. I must remain open-minded to receive it. I'm ready for this season to end. I'm tired of crying. I'm tired of feeling vulnerable. I'm tired of social media. My timeline looks like the Houston Chronicle obituary section. People keep dying. Or, am I just more sensitive to death?

We were barely into the new year when I received a call from the prosecutor. He said he would like to speak with my mom and I in preparation for trial. I really wanted to protect my mom. I told the prosecutor she was very emotional during the holidays and that Fabian's 30th Birthday was approaching. I told him I would only bring her if he felt it was absolutely necessary. He said he really wanted her to be in attendance.

January 10, 2018 – My mom and I met with the prosecutor yesterday. I can remember him saying "My thought is the 1st shot was fatal, but he emptied the cartridge anyway. I hate to speak of it this way, but it was nothing less than an execution. He's a murderer who has talked about his addiction to drugs. I've listened to his jail calls and he uses racial slurs. His ex has said they committed a robbery together for marijuana." I sat up nice and tall, fighting my emotions. My mom cried at the sound of my brother's name. Lord knows I wanted to do the same. I couldn't look at her. I had to be strong. I also wanted to reply, "but this is the person who has been granted bond on two different occasions?" My brother may have been 130 pounds soaking wet...you could get anything you wanted from him with no bullet. Why did Tyler Green empty the cartridge? What was he trying to prove? What was he trying to prevent? Probably the possibility of my brother living to tell his side of the story.

I'm sure the homicide detectives and prosecutor had grown weary with my questioning. I had asked them during several different conversations WHY had Tyler Green murdered my brother? I asked several of Fabe's friends and several people who claimed to know the murderer. I had a good understanding of the aggravating and mitigating circumstances, but my question remained unanswered. I was told that Tyler was refusing to talk. Of course, that was his right, but for me, that said a lot.

January 23, 2018 - I feel like a damn detective. I'm working so hard to prove my brother was murdered and Tyler Christian Green is guilty. As if they don't have evidence. Eye witnesses, surveillance footage, cell tower data, and the damn body! I don't know what more they would need to keep this monster off the streets. The defense attorney, Stephen Aslett, lied and said that I told him, "On February 19, 2017, Fabian said I'll be back, I have to f#%^ some people up." I understand why most victims and families reject communication with the defense. Stephen could add another s and remove the "lett" from his name. Who does he think I am? He thinks I'm stupid. Fabian hadn't shown anything but smiles and peace during our time together that day. He posted an Instagram video just moments before he was killed. I gave some of them more respect than they deserved. The prosecutor pissed me the hell off because he and Stephen supposedly had that conversation earlier today. He and I have talked enough for him to know that I know better to even provide an opportunity for the defense to make up such a lie. What was the context of the conversation that made Stephen comfortable enough to make that allegation about me to the person who is representing my family and me? The prosecutor didn't call me until hours later. He asked if I said it as if he actually believed it! Stephen should be disbarred! As if the prosecutor doesn't know the games courtroom actors play, I went back and forth pleading my case. Of course, I didn't say that. I'm so confused. The prosecutor is the one who told me it may be worth it to have a conversation with the defense. Now, he seems to be questioning me. My trust issues are resurfacing. Is anybody on my side? Only God. I need to release this, so it doesn't consume or confuse me. Trial is in 6 days. The prosecutor told me jury selection may be expedited to this Friday. He responded with information about the "system" and how quickly the date could change. I told him I want justice! He ended by thanking me for the conversation.

    The prosecutor was a master communicator. During my time with him, he never mirrored my anger or frustration. The defense attorney, Stephen Aslett, was playing a scandalous game and I did not know how long it had gone on. On Friday January 20, 2018, the defense attorney called and proceeded to bad mouth the prosecutor. My guess is that he, too, had seen my advocacy work via social media and my disproval with the justice system. So, he either wanted to serve as a trigger, so I would portray myself as the stereotypical mad, black woman, or he actually thought I was stupid enough to believe I could count on him to provide what the system had failed to provide. Stephen threw subtle shade. He said, "Keaton is good. Even though he doesn't always answer; he's busy." I responded by telling him that I could not even imagine the demands of Keaton's position. Stephen made several other stupid comments that are not worth typing. However, when he told me, "I am here for you. Do you have any questions for me at this point?" I was triggered! I told him I understood he had a job to do and that was to defend the monster who murdered my brother. I informed him that I also had a job to do and that was to be my deceased brother's voice. I informed Stephen that he failed me when he instructed Tyler Green to sit next to me (of all places) in the courtroom. I was appalled by his negligence! I could not believe I had sat next to the devil who murdered my brother. I felt like a chump for having done nothing! I did not do or say anything. I wanted to ask him why he had murdered my brother? I was so shocked that I could not.

January 24, 2018 – I was in class when I received a call from the prosecutor stating that jury selection would begin tomorrow!! I wasn't ready. I thought I was. I thought I was ready to complete trial and go on with my life. I prayed several times and told God that I would trust Him and refrain from worrying about the outcome. I knew this would create challenges for my parents to request off and for my family to arrive from Mississippi. Today was hard. Last night was rough, even after bible study. Mentally, I'm somewhere between my next level and a mental breakdown. We have yet to receive a call from victim services regarding trial. I thought my cousin would be able to support my mom during trial, but she has no baby sitter. She mentioned that she'll just bring her 5-year-old daughter to court. I highly discouraged taking her into what is bound to be a very traumatic experience. I mean, it has been for me! I could not wait to get to my car after school to scream! I called my Great-Grandmama and just dumped it all on her. We cried together and shared stories of pain and God's goodness... just like I knew we would. I knew it was a bit much for her at the age of 87. But, I had no one else to call who I thought would meet me where I was. I texted an old friend who I had also spent most of my New Year break with. I was impressed with how prompt and supportive he was. I couldn't reach anyone else. One of my mentors didn't answer. Another was extremely dry and offered no assistance. The prosecutor didn't answer. Another attorney who I provided pro bono services for didn't answer. I've been here before. God wants me to know that it's just He and I. He has already won it. I just need to show up and walk in it. My patience is thin. I want to be comforted, and I am searching for comfort in all the wrong places. I was hungry and calling people for answers they did not have and could not provide. My Great-grandmama told me to call my dad, because he has the Flu. I don't mind calling for that reason, but I don't want to discuss trial. I know he will support me if I need him too, but I feel terrible and undeserving because I have not supported him much after my uncle's death. They buried my uncle on Fabe's birthday. I did not know how to articulate to anyone, except my grandmother, that my heart and mind could not handle attending a funeral on Fabian's birthday. My grieving was already interrupted by the call that my Uncle Reb had died. My mom invited me to bible study; she knew something was wrong. I declined the offer and felt bad afterwards. Lord, this has tested my faith and shaken up my foundation. God said to me, "Don't play me. This does not speak to who I am. It speaks to what you believe. Your response is doubtful and disappointing." **Lord, I am sorry.** *Teach me to do your will, your way. Considering my instability, Lord, I just want to thank you for all that I have not lost in this season.*

Trial

On Thursday January 25, 2018, I attended jury selection. Considering the demographics of Harris County, the prospective jurors were not as diverse as I expected. There was an overwhelming majority of Caucasian individuals. I could count the others on one hand. Immediately, I thought about my family and friends. It was discouraging to admit that most people I knew sought ways to be excused from jury duty. I heard people talk about how their absence, although excused, would impact their job. I have also heard people refuse to tackle downtown parking and traffic to attend jury duty. I did not see jury duty as merely an opportunity, but as an obligation to one another. How could we complain about a broken system while refusing to exercise the rights we have?

January 26, 2018 - Court did not begin as scheduled today. I sensed a disregard for others and their time since the first court appearance. I feel good, and that's a little scary. I feel a radical kinda faith. I'm changing. I feel guilty for feeling relaxed. I do not want my brother to look down from heaven and think I take this situation lightly. But, I don't feel heavy at all. I feel relieved that trial has started. I got a good look at the murderer's parents and what appears to be a sister or a significant other. It's hard to tell based on her interaction with his parents. Some of the details they've mentioned prove that this offense was worse than I imagined…but as bizarre as the offenses on Law and Order. After murdering my brother, Tyler Green's adoptive mother told him to come and move his car from in front of her home. She never told him to contact law enforcement or turn himself in. That tree is potentially as dangerous as that apple. There is proof that the murderer never turned himself in, and he spoke to his mom several times on different dates before he was apprehended. They discussed the murder, and she provided advice that did not include instructions or suggestions for him to turn himself in. His mom was exposed for providing inconsistent information. In addition to lying under oath, she indicated some aiding and abetting. She got on my nerves. She cried and gave the jury a "sick puppy dog" look during her testimony. My sister stated that she recognized the murderer as Fabe's ex-coworker at Applebee's. I was made aware of this early on, and some of the employees at Applebee's were assets to this case. Several of them stated they were able to identify the murderer as soon as the surveillance video was released by the media. One employee stated that she called Tyler and asked him, "Why did you kill Fabian?" She said Tyler responded by denying and added that he had been out of town with his dad over the weekend. Another employee stated that she didn't believe that allegation because Tyler mentioned being homeless. I know we will win. Being an advocate against gun violence, it's difficult to sit and listen to the Green Family (specifically Tyler's adoptive Father) discuss hunting and their gun use as a sport. He talked about how early Tyler was trained to use guns and several different weapons that Tyler may have had access to because they went hunting together. Tyler murdered my brother like he was an animal. Our family dynamics are definitely different. Fabe was not allowed to have toy guns growing up. My mom did not play that! My dad had a weapon, but it was strictly for protection. I saw it on accident under the driver seat. My dad looked so ashamed when I saw the gun for the first time. He never flashed it. He never mentioned hunting or shooting anything for sport. Fabe wasn't allowed to have bb guns, toy guns, nothing! My mom didn't even like water guns. But, this family keeps attempting to justify the murderer's actions by mentioning his gun usage as a sport or hobby. They also mentioned that the murderer collects knifes and hot wheels. I walked away still not knowing why my brother was shot five times, and he was unarmed. Why would someone be in a strip center in a suburban area wearing a black trench

Trial

coat, black shades, and a black fedora carrying a gun? Oh, and just a reminder, this took place around 2:00 PM on a beautiful Sunday afternoon. The Green family mentioned the murderer's drug addiction in what appeared to be an attempt to solicit sympathy from the jury. This is sooo dangerous! How much worse could it get? Here is a 24-year-old battling drug addiction who has access to guns. I can't understand how he made it in and out of several businesses within the strip center because his attire included a black trench coat, black shades, and a black fedora. I can't get over his outfit because I confirmed the weather was 81/73° F on 02/19/2017. Today, the defense attorney said, "That's just how he liked to dress." I have gone to every court appearance (except those conducted inside the jail), and the killer never showed up to court dressed like that. I have seen Tyler and the Green family in the lobby, the elevator, and the courtroom. I have witnessed them laughing and smiling. They seem supportive and unusually happy considering the circumstances. I wonder if the smiles and laughter indicate the murderer and his family have more faith in a favorable outcome than me. Lord, if that is the case, shame on me! They never once attempted to apologize. They were probably instructed to not speak to us. Despite the instructions, my heart would not allow me to sit next to a hurting family and not offer sympathy.

Before trial began, I was informed that I was selected as a fact witness for the case. The prosecutor also asked my mom to testify. I was the last family member to see Fabe alive. I was also informed that I would be prohibited from sitting in the courtroom during certain parts of trial to prevent my testimony from being influenced by others. I was concerned about missing some of the testimonies and statements made by both the prosecutor and the defense attorney, but I was even more concerned about not being able to provide emotional support to my family during this traumatic event. On day one, my mom ran out of the courtroom screaming and holding her face. For the first time in 12 months, she saw an enlarged photo of my brother's dead body with markings that indicated bullet entry and exit points. THERE WAS NOTHING I COULD DO! I did not think she deserved this experience. My mom walked out of trial and said, "I'm going to get my mama." She wanted the support. She needed the support. And my Grandmother wanted to provide support, but the drive was too far and there was no sense in mentioning a flight! I could not believe my mom was seriously going to pick my grandmother up and return before trial resumed on Monday. I knew she was already experiencing mental distress, but that 12-hour roundtrip drive was physically demanding. I decided not to join her. I needed to focus and get some work done. I was learning so much more about the criminal justice system. I even learned that whether a murder was premeditated was irrelevant for a first-degree murder charge in Texas. Unfortunately, none of that would be covered on my upcoming tests or assignments.

January 29, 2018 – I'm stuck in the lobby. I'm tired of being in such proximity to the murderer's family. But, I don't want to go too far and end up missing an opportunity to return to the courtroom. I am so relieved to see the victim services coordinator. She offered to sit with me in the lobby, but I pretended to be okay. I told her I would really appreciate her checking on my mom since I couldn't be with her. The victim services coordinator is doing the best she can to keep me updated. I'm sure she's gotten her 10,000 steps in for the day. She must have seen the anxiousness all over my face. She said they had gone through "lots of technical stuff". She said the following individuals took the stand: cell phone data analyst, medical examiner, and the ballistics expert.
This afternoon, I was allowed to enter the courtroom. Keri Livingston (Tyler Green's girlfriend now and at the time of

the murder) said that on the night of the murder, she cooked dinner and Tyler vomited. She said she knew something was wrong, but she thought he was vomiting because of the Thai food she cooked. This all seems so unreal. It's hard for me to fathom murdering a man and returning home to have dinner with my family. The pain I consistently experience, because I miss my brother so much, reminds me that this is real. It's hard to comprehend, but, I can feel it. I guess Keri hadn't seen the surveillance video that surfaced on the news and social media? Others who knew the murderer reported they recognized Tyler even with his trench coat, shades, and fedora. The prosecutor referenced four of the murderer's jail calls. During these calls, Keri Livingston called Tyler "a fucking liar." During one of the calls, the murderer responded, "maybe I lie sometimes." Keri has two children; neither of them were fathered by the murderer. However, she has been in a custody battle since her father's son found out Tyler committed a murder. This was probably the least shocking detail I heard all day. The trace evidence expert confirmed (and others) that there was no weapon in Fabe's vehicle. The trace evidence expert also confirmed there were no signs of a struggle or self-defense. This also wasn't shocking. I had never known my brother to carry a weapon. Fabe knew how to defend himself if he needed to, but he had a small frame. Tyler was larger than my brother. Therefore, I knew it was very unlikely that my brother initiated an argument or a physical altercation with a guy larger than him who happened to be wearing a black trench coat, black fedora, and black shades.

Tyler's girlfriend, Keri, proved to be just as negligent as Tyler's mother. During trial, Keri admitted her bullets were missing, and her gun had been moved. The detectives confirmed that Tyler's clothing, containing small blood splatters, was found in Keri's closet behind a clothing hamper. The prosecutor mentioned that Keri's sister contacted Crime stoppers. Walking out of the courtroom, we all had slightly different reactions. My dad said the obscene photographs of my brother's corpse gave him closure. He said seeing the photos helped him to understand that there was nothing EMS could do to save my brother's life. As a practitioner, he wondered how effective the medical professionals had been. I was upset; I felt that Tyler's mother and girlfriend were criminally responsible for failing to use common sense to say the least. Their testimonies were difficult to sit through.

On Tuesday January 30, 2018, everything I experienced that day felt extremely unusual, but I wanted to resume my usual routine. I went straight to bible study after court. I was happy to see my church family, but I sat alone in the back to avoid expectations. I knew I needed a word from the Lord, and I felt an obligation to worship. I did not journal that day. I felt so overwhelmed, but I was unable to describe my thoughts and feelings with words. I was so tired of seeing my mom cry. My grandmother joined us for court that Monday. She is one of the toughest women I know, but there were moments when she had to walk out. I was worried about her. She gasped while hearing the offense details and seeing the gruesome photos of shots to her grandson's body and his blood splattered throughout the pictures. I will never forget cleaning Fabe's car and finding his white, USB cord that contained splatters of his blood. After seeing several pictures of the gunshot wounds to his upper torso, the USB cord made a little more sense. I fought to hold back tears and screams. I did not want the murderer or his family to gain any satisfaction from seeing me collapse. Once the judge announced the lunch break, everyone started to slowly exit the courtroom. I could hear people discussing their lunch options. The victim services coordinator stayed behind to see what my family and I planned to eat for lunch. I remember seeing the left door of the courtroom swing, indicating the last person (other than us) had exited. I collapsed. The tears were pouring. With all my strength, I tried to remain silent. I started shaking profusely. My head was pounding. My heart was aching. I inflicted so much more pain on myself by not walking out and taking mental breaks like my Grandma. I closed my eyes in attempt to avoid the bright lights, only to replay the photos of my brother's frail body and the tattoo of my name. My mom I and reversed roles. She did not just display a refreshed strength, she became exactly who I needed her to be at that moment and covered me.

January 31, 2018- Today, we started with closing arguments. The defense went first. The defense attorney told the jury, "The only thing Tyler has ever done was shot and killed Fabian. Let's not judge him on the worst 5-6 seconds of he and Fabian's life." How sick and insensitive! Had he not known Tyler was on probation at the time of the murder? Did he not know that Tyler had violated his conditions of bond supervision? Had he not listened to Tyler's jail calls? It's no wonder he's able to represent a murderer with so much confidence; the defense attorney's character is questionable! He spent a substantial amount of time discrediting the state's witnesses and evidence. He referred to Tyler as "a 25-year-old kid." Tyler is a murderer! While the defense attorney consistently insulted the intelligence of everyone in the courtroom, the prosecutor appealed to the jury by referring to common sense. The prosecutor stated that Fabian was murdered a year ago and the murderer had failed to tell anyone why. Until today. The defense (to include Tyler Green, Stephen Aslett, and all who testified on their behalf) was deceitful and cold during cross examination. It's so hard to forgive a person who refuses to accept responsibility. But, I understand my freedom is attached to this forgiveness. My family spent so much time with the victim services coordinator that our conversations were no longer just about the trial and court proceedings.

Murdered by a Christian, On a Sunday

We appreciated her peace, so we discussed family, hobbies, favorite vacation spots, etc... After a little while, I got distracted. I felt myself relinquishing desires and concerns for trial and trusting that God would take care of my family.

The judge called for a break. The arguments had become extremely heated as both the prosecutor and the defense attorney knew they had one last opportunity to plead two totally different cases. The prosecutor provided a substantial amount of evidence pointing to Tyler's drug addiction, manipulation and deceit towards his family and friends, and racial prejudices that could have contributed to his malicious actions. The amount of evidence was increasing faster than I could process it. I was so disturbed after seeing photos of my brother's corpse displayed on an overhead projector for all to see. I remember wondering how he looked so peaceful in the casket, but so uncomfortable on the photographs provided by the medical examiner? During his homegoing celebration, Fabe looked genuinely peaceful, not like an embalmer had altered his facial expression for esthetic purposes. I had not eaten much in days. We were in court an average of eight hours each day. Before and after trial, the last thing on my mind was eating. This break was no different. My family and I needed to stay nearby because the judge could resume or reset at any moment. We paid to park for court and would likely have to pay for parking at the nearby restaurants, so it did not make sense to drive anywhere. The victim services coordinator informed us that food was available inside the courthouse. I figured the Green family may have been told the same. After several hours with them in the courtroom and lobby, I did not want to have lunch with them. I wondered if Tyler posed a threat to himself or anyone else at that point? We were breaking for lunch, but he was facing a conviction for first degree murder and up to 99 years in prison.

When court resumed, the defense called Tyler's "childhood friend" to the stand as a character witness. A Hispanic gentleman approached the bench and testified about how "good" of a friend Tyler was. The gentleman was small in frame, like my brother. He seemed very nervous. He stuttered a little and his voice became shaky. I must say, as a fact witness, approaching the bench was enough to make me shake like a leaf on a tree. But, I continued with a boldness that could have only come from the Lord. I was even more encouraged when I looked out and saw the homicide detectives sitting near my family, because they also wanted justice to be served! I wonder how Tyler's friend felt to testify on his behalf after hearing the jail calls where Tyler described his racist attitude towards African-Americans and Hispanics? During another call, Tyler seemed very upset with his mom about something. He cursed her and told her, "When God created you, I guess He didn't give you a fucking brain!" Nevertheless, several of Tyler's family and friends mentioned his church volunteer work during their testimonies! How manipulative of them to think these elaborate descriptions of his church involvement deemed him innocent of murder in the eyes of the jury. Meanwhile, I thought about how the murderer would be allowed to exercise his right to freedom of religion within Texas Department of Criminal Justice. Fair enough! I worked as an intake office, so I knew he could even keep his beard if he claims it serves a religious purpose. If their allegations were true, I would have to find peace in knowing my brother was murdered on a Sunday, by a Christian.

After about two hours of deliberation, the bailiff entered and said, "All rise for the jury." I became so weak that I could barely comply. I looked at my mom, grandmother, and the victim services coordinator. The prosecutor looked at me. My family and I were terrified. The prosecutor and victim services coordinator looked hopeful. I was shocked that the homicide detectives were still present.

This case had consumed us all. I prayed so loud and courageously on the inside that I would not be surprised if others told me they could hear me. I bowed my head and closed my eyes.

I begged God for victory. I apologized for my unbelief. I reminded Him that He said I am above and never below, victory belongs to Him, and He'd make a footstool out of my enemies. I reminded myself that His grace is sufficient for me, His power lives in me, and He said He'd never leave me or forsake me. I went on and on, desperately.

Amid my prayer and praise, I heard the judge say, "Guilty of 1st degree murder." I was even more weak. I burst into tears and within seconds, the victim services coordinator was there to interrupt my fall. My God had shown up to fulfill His promises. The truth is, God is in covenant with his word. So, whether I deserved it is irrelevant! He did it because He said He would do it! I was so occupied with faith that the fear that had tormented me for the past year fled the scene. There was reciprocity of hugs and high fives. The judge called for another break as we transitioned from the punishment phase into the sentencing phase of trial. The first person I shared the news with was my other mom, Tameka Clayton. She provided an immense amount of support during trial. When I was unable to journal or speak, I sent her gruesome details that were disclosed to process my experience throughout the day. She was my pro bono therapist. I confided in her because I was concerned that my mental health was declining by the day, and I could trust that she would not repeat the information. This news of a guilty verdict also included my gratitude for her support.

By 7:00 PM that evening, the judge stated the jury had yet to agree on a punishment, so court would resume at 9:00 AM. Although, I really wanted to know that day, I realized that for a charge that carries 2 to 99 years, I would probably need an extended amount of time to decide on punishment too. That is an enormous gap! I could not imagine the pressure experienced by the jury. There were a few more testimonies that may have impacted the jury. The defense attorney and the murderer's mother bragged about how great of a worker Tyler had been since the murder. He was working from home, for the same company as his mother, recruiting health care professionals. Once on the stand, his boss admitted he could mostly speak to what Tyler's mother said about him because he and Tyler had limited, infrequent communication or contact. This horror story took another turn when the prosecutor called a confident looking Caucasian woman to the stand. I consider her to be one our greatest assets to the case. She identified herself as Chelsea Murphy, the wife of Tyler Christian Green! Chelsea stated she and the murderer were separated at the time of the murder. She admitted their relationship was infested with drug usage, and they attended rehab together. She added that she was clean and so much better since she left him. She testified that the murderer had committed other crimes and stole money from her. She mentioned that Tyler was mean to his family, especially his mom, but they always tried to help him. In addition to solidifying some of my speculations, Chelsea's testimony included some details that I will never forget. She stated that Tyler's clothing in the surveillance video did not shock her because he admired mobsters. She added "He said that one thing he had always wanted to do was kill a man and watch the blood gush from his body." Right then, I knew this battle was not mine; it's the Lord's. For the past year of my life, I made this all so personal. Chelsea's comment indicated that had it not been my brother, it would have been someone else's brother. The murderer was on a mission, and my big brother just happened to be along his path.

February 1, 2018 – Almost one year to the day my brother was killed. Today, Tyler Christian Green was sentenced to 50 years in prison for 1st degree murder. I delivered the

Murdered by a Christian, On a Sunday

Victim Impact Statement. His family walked out as soon as I approached the bench. I guess they didn't want to hear anything I had to say. They were no longer smiling and laughing. Now, two families were hurting. A guilty verdict and 50 years would not revive that corpse of my brother that was displayed so many times. For everything my brother could not say, I gave my speech and looked the murderer directly in his eyes the entire time. My fear was gone. Besides, God didn't give me that anyway.

"It doesn't matter if you don't see God, as long as the hell you're going through sees him" – Dr. Jasmin Sculark

VII.   Church Hurt

About one month after trial, I was wondering what was next. I knew that winners did not celebrate a victory for too long. I felt the season was shifting, and I needed to get going while I had momentum. I was so adamant about allowing my brother to live through me. During my spring break, I took a few quick trips to places I thought he would enjoy. As a full-time student, I was unable to travel as often and as far as I would like. I promised myself that even in familiar places, I would experience the unfamiliar! I went to my brother's grave; I had so much to tell him. I remember it being such a beautiful day. That smile on the picture that his grave marker held was contagious. I noticed his receding hairline…the topic of so many of my jokes. Oh, how I miss him! I asked him to watch over me. I trusted that he would. He always had.

Once the semester resumed, I noticed that I needed frequent mental breaks throughout the day. I juggled between plans for the future and pain from the past. When I felt overwhelmed, I walked away. Physically removing myself seemed to help. I really enjoyed listening to music. I observed nature more; I found beauty in God's creations. I imagined my life beyond the brokenness, and that was enough to provoke happiness and inner peace.

Self-care and boundary setting were my priorities, but I continued to struggle with both. I missed my distant family; I really wanted to be with my siblings and my nephew. But, I needed to be in Houston, because I also missed my church family. Failure to attend one service left me feeling empty for days. Well, I had missed several. It was not my intent to forsake the opportunity to fellowship with others, but I needed some one-on-one with my creator. Some days, I had to sit in his presence and not say a word. My weekday commute provided ample time for me to worship. I could not control what happened throughout the day, but I could control how I started each one. Every day, I sought ways to be productive. I mentioned that my brother depended on me for so much, so I searched for ways to be dependable for others. In my saying "yes" to so much more, I was drifting further from church, again. Sundays became catch up days that were used to pay the price for my difficulty focusing and procrastination during the week. I was so distracted on Tuesdays that I did not realize the day or time until it was already after 7 PM. I either attended bible study late or missed it altogether. I was given some life-changing opportunities, but I questioned whether they were sent by God. I knew He would not send opportunities that pulled me away from him. I made small changes in my schedule to assure my relationship with God would always come first.

As difficult as my graduate coursework was, I was relieved that my school was located on the third floor of South Main Baptist church. No matter how busy I became, I was certain I would encounter believers and be reminded of God's goodness at least two days each week. I loved the scripture that was displayed throughout the building. The church is holy ground, and I respect it as such. I believed I could bring all my baggage there, and for anything I was willing to surrender, God was willing to accept it.

I chose to pursue a graduate degree from Baylor University because of their emphasis on faith and practice. During my professional career, I was always required to separate the two. I was excited about integrating faith to better serve individuals, no matter their faith. As a graduate assistant for the program, I was often on campus (at the church) for 6-7 days each week, unlike other students who only attended 2 days each week for classes. I was grateful for the opportunity to study and work inside of a church. I thought that was another indicator of God's love for me.

On March 28, 2018, I pulled into the church parking lot around 8:20 AM for my 9:00 AM Research class. I exited my driver's side and walked around to the front, passenger side of my car to grab my backpack, lunch kit, and purse. From the passenger side of my car, I could see my colleague, Whitney. She was also on the passenger side of her car grabbing her bags. I could see that Whitney was balancing her cellphone between her face and right ear. I proceeded towards her to see if she needed help carrying her things. She denied needing my assistance, so I waited patiently for her. In the parking spot to my left, I could see another colleague sitting in her car with her car still powered on. I observed my instructor entering the church, and to my right, I saw another colleague on the sidewalk headed towards the entrance of the church. Several other individuals where entering, but I did not recognize them. I assumed they were church staff or members. I asked Whitney, "Do you need any help carrying your stuff?" She interrupted her telephone conversation to reply, "No," and continued to gather her things.

Within seconds, a green Fiat pulled up perpendicular to the rear of Whitney's vehicle. A Caucasian male (who I had never seen before) was driving and asked me, "What are you looking for?" His tone was very rude, and I noticed he was wearing a hat that had several patches. I could not decipher if the patches were consistent with law enforcement, military, or security. In shock, I replied, "What did you ask me?" I thought I had misunderstood or misheard the man. His question seemed awkward, because I was not looking for anything. I was only there for a minute or two waiting for Whitney. The male responded, "What are you looking for? Where are you going?" I was confused. I had been in and out of the church since August 2017 but had never seen this man or been asked these questions. Still trying to figure out who this man was, I replied "Who are you and why did you pull over here?" He replied, "I'm security and I have a right to supervise this property and ask you what you're doing." His tone was stern and accusatory. His attire and attitude were much different than the church facility attendants I encountered previously. I asked, "What do you mean, what am I looking for? I'm here all the time, and I've never seen you..." The man interrupted and began to speak. My colleague, Whitney, interjected and said "We're students here. We attend Baylor University. Why did you come over here?" His tone was a little less rude and he replied, "I have a right to..." I said "Sir, what is your name because this is unacceptable. I've seen other people walk into the building, and you didn't stop any of them. I will be speaking to someone about this." He replied, "My name is Chief, and you go right ahead. I've been here 38 years...." I said "Okay, this is ridiculous." The man drove off.

This was one of my safe places! I kept a blanket in the file cabinet because I was often there from open to close. Why had this guy stopped me, but no one else? Whitney and I proceeded into the church, and the man followed us. On the third floor, we walked into the area where the administrative offices were located. Whitney explained to the receptionist that an incident had taken place in the parking lot, and we needed to speak with someone. The receptionist, who we met and spoke to several times, explained that we needed to call a number for support and proceeded to provide the number. Whitney and I explained that if someone else was in the building and available, we really needed to speak with someone at that time. I thought, "This is a church! When someone mentions that something happened on the property, you think an adequate response is to provide a phone number?" She never asked for any details! I really felt my safety had been jeopardized! Within seconds, the man from the parking lot walked into the waiting area. In the same rude, argumentative tone, the man said, "I've been here 38 years supervising this property and I have a right to ask..." Whitney was seated while he was standing, and he leaned forward (closer to her) while he spoke. I watched in disbelief as her personal space was being invaded. I became nervous when I realized that the man followed us to the third floor to continue his argument. I replied, "Sir, it's not what you asked, it's how you asked. You were very rude. You stopped me and questioned me, but I didn't see you question anyone else." At this point, I was still questioning who the man was, because I had not observed the other three security officers (who I saw on a regular basis) wear a hat or uniform with patches like this man. Also, unlike the other security officers, this man had a utility belt that contained mace and some other items I could not identify. From my seat, I could not confirm if he was carrying a firearm, but I feared that he was. Within moments, the receptionist motioned for Whitney and me to go back and speak with Brad Jernberg. The man from the parking lot also went back, but he stopped near the departmental mailboxes while we continued down the hall.

Brad Jernberg's title is Minister of Administration for Operations. During the conversation with Brad, Whitney and I described the incident from the parking lot and informed him that "Chief" had also followed us to the third floor where he continued arguing and justifying his behavior. "Chief" was just steps away near the mailboxes, but Brad never attempted to include him in the meeting. Brad apologized for Chief's actions and stated that was the first time he had ever received a complaint like that about Chief. I replied, "And today was my first time seeing this man." I reassured Brad that as a graduate assistant and student, I'm at the church sometimes seven days each week and have never been treated like that by security or any other staff member. He reiterated that our claims were inconsistent with his interaction and comments he had heard about Chief. Brad asked me for specific statements made by Chief to be relayed to Chief's supervisor. Brad stated that the situation would be handled. I informed Brad that on the previous Saturday, I spoke with Pastor Wells at the Micah 6:8 conference and he invited me to attend worship service. I informed Brad that the Pastor's invitation was inconsistent with how I had been treated in the parking lot. I also added, "I wonder if the

Pastor knows this is going on? This man pulled up in his personal car and attempted to interrogate me. I wonder who else he's treated like this? He bragged about being here for 30+ years, but what a shame!" Brad denied having an incident report we could complete at that time. He stated that when the report was completed, Whitney and I would not have access to it because the security officer was an employee of the church. Throughout the conversation, he reiterated we were Baylor Students, and Baylor is a tenant of the church.

All along, I thought there was a partnership with Baylor University and South Main Baptist Church. There is a significant difference between a tenant and a partner, and Brad made that clear in his demeanor towards us. I asked Brad if anyone would follow up with me and he replied, "if you email me, I'll have your email, and I'll follow up with you." Brad provided his business card and stated that he was "okay" with me contacting the university and the pastor. He stated that the Pastor was not available at that time but provided an email for the Pastor. I continued to share my frustration. Whitney and I thanked Brad before exiting. Brad attempted to minimize the incident every time he opened his mouth. I left his office more disoriented than I entered. I am not sure if he realized it or not, but his immediate reaction to protect chief was obvious. Brad covered Chief with a white sheet…he talked about this man as if he had no blemishes…I couldn't help but wonder if Chief had a white hood somewhere nearby.

Around 3:50 PM on that same day, I was exiting the church with another colleague. I did not think it was wise or safe for me to be alone on the premises of South Main Baptist Church. Henry (a security officer who I was familiar with) stopped me and asked what happened between Chief and I. The fact that he knew something happened indicated a discussion had already taken place. I replied, "I was in the parking lot this morning, and an officer who I have never seen before, pulled up to me and basically interrogated me for no reason. Other people were walking in the parking lot and into the church, and I didn't see him stop anyone else. I'm wearing a Baylor University shirt, carrying a backpack and other things, but I feel like he was profiling me." Henry replied, "Chief is a very good guy. He's been here for 38 years. He thought you were homeless." I was offended and in disbelief, and I am sure my facial expression displayed both. I said nothing else. Henry concluded by saying "I'm not trying to make excuses for him." I replied, "Okay," and proceeded to my car.

During my afternoon commute, I was disappointed by what had taken place in the parking lot with Chief, and by both Brad and Henry's response. Even if I were homeless, for heaven's sake this is a church! I believe we should respect the dignity and worth of all people, not excluding homeless people. My heart hurt for the homeless population near Main Street and Wheeler Avenue, just feet away from the church. None of this made sense to me. I got out of a car, wore a backpack, carried a lunch kit, and a laptop bag. I happened to be in the parking lot of the church where the Baylor campus is located, wearing an ash grey shirt that read "Baylor Bears" in large, block letters. Homelessness has no look, but, they felt I looked the part. How much more difficult will it be to transform nonbelievers into believers if we treat them like this in the parking lot of the church?

To be continued….

Murdered by a Christian, On a Sunday

"I was glad when they said unto me, 'Let us go unto the house of the Lord!" Psalm 122:1

VIII.   Life After Death

I'm still here. One year later. I can hear the phenomenal Mya Angelou saying, "Still I rise." No matter what your religious beliefs are, I strongly recommend submitting your life to a higher power. The surrender that my faith requires relieved me of the pressure to fix everything that has gone wrong. I know these are not my battles to fight. As they would say at the church I grew up in, "When I think, I thank." When I think about all God has brought me through, the thoughts make my knees weak. And I do not fight that weakness because I understand that when I am weak, my God is strong. Being on my knees is my favorite position for worship. I know I am not worthy. I am nothing more than filthy rags undeserving of His presence. I conclude that I was questioning God because I did not fully understand who I was or my purpose.

The last place on my agenda was church. With assignments piling up, the last book on my list was the bible. I was so jacked up in expecting to see God without seeking Him. I waited so long for God to speak to me as He had all the parking lot prophets at church. When He finally spoke to me, it was not empathetic or reassuring, so I tried avoiding Him. He sounded more like a Father than I expected. My great-grandmama, with her unfailing love, shoved God in my face every time we spoke. Her words were a pathway to His presence. She helped me to see the very one I questioned was carrying me through it all.

I have asked God for so much in my lifetime. After experiencing tragedy, I blamed myself and thought maybe I did not realize I was sacrificing my brother with all my requests. The fact that I was the one who woke him up on February 19, 2017 only made matters worse. Every time I asked God to give me more, I had unconsciously agreed to give Him more. I used to beg God to take my life to the next level. I cried at the alter for 52 Sundays and 52 Tuesdays promising to honor him with my life. I was exposed to so much greatness, and it was all proof that there was so much more to life than I ever imagined. I always wanted to win, but not just for me. I wanted to win for everybody attached to me, especially my brother because he knew how low we started. While I was asking for more, it is as if God was sitting high, looking low, and responding, "Well, how bad do you want it? Do you really mean what you say?" From one incident to another, I repeated, "this is the hardest thing I have ever had to do." On my mission to live extraordinarily, I decided I would keep going no matter what. For every new level, I faced a new devil. Writing this book was no different. This is one of the hardest things I have ever had to do. I have relived the trauma, reread documents, and reviewed social media posts. Being transparent has required me to revisit some of the beginning stages of the grief cycle. I hid this project for an entire year because I did not want others to dictate how I depict my story.

Over the course of one year, I lost my brother, some material possessions, and friendships I never imagined losing. By this chapter, my thoughts and feelings towards my brother should be clear. I have learned to live life on the simplest of terms, and I understand there may always be an area of lack in my life. Material possessions do not make or break me. Looking back, it is challenging for me to explain what happened between my friends and I while respecting that they have their translation of the story. My tolerance for negativity decreased. I did not have time to beg anyone to remain in my life who did not want to be here. I love and miss my friends, but they did a much better job at outlining my flaws than realizing how good of a friend I sought to be over the years. My family and I have an unbreakable bond that emerged from this tragedy. My mom and I have an amazing relationship! Our conversations may start with jokes about things that only Fabian could get away with, but end in tears because all we have left are memories. I often pray that my surviving siblings know that I love them just as much. I cherish them more than ever before, but I cannot even describe to them the relationship that Fabe and I had. It was different because he and I spent more time together. Of course, we experienced sibling rivalry, but Fabe would not allow me to be mad at him for more than a few hours. It used to aggravate me so bad because I wanted to be mad at him and show him how tough I was. He was more concerned with showing me he could make me laugh and that he loved me no matter what. My brother's death impacted the dynamics of every relationship I have maintained. I evaluate who and what is receiving my time…what matters and what does not. Fabe took so many of my secrets to his grave with him. I often waddle in tears about the goals he was not able to accomplish (being a husband, father, traveling, and launching his business). But, then I am reminded that he touched so many lives in 29 short years and did have some extraordinary experiences!

    The latter half of this book details the mental and spiritual shift that was required for me to persevere. So instead of asking "why", I started asking, "what now?" Lord, what do I do with these broken pieces? My life has taken on a whole new meaning; I set goals with a sense of urgency. My questioning resulted in a much greater understanding of Christianity. Nevertheless, death is so real. I still struggle with accepting that it is a part of life. Often, I think about the people I love most and become devastated at the thought of losing them. I understand it is going to happen, but not knowing when robs me of the ability to brace myself. I have admitted that I am guilty of being a hypocrite at times. I have asked God to help my unbelief. Death is something I continue to question him about. How ready should I be? Although I have worked so hard to develop coping skills, I still don't know how I will respond in the face of death. I pray that God gives me threescore years and ten, plus many years of grace, but I do not want to be left here all alone. My quality of life will be impacted every time I lose a loved one. I have preexisting attachment issues that are agitated by death.

I was taught that I am a foreigner in this land, and God has prepared a place for me. Yet, when my brother died, I was tested on everything I have ever been taught. Initially, I failed; thank God for retests. I acted like my family was exempt from the troubles of this world. I acted like God had not given his only son, who knew no sin, but became sin, just for my brother (and all other believers) to have eternal life. In selfishness, I was trying to hold my brother from Heaven. I wanted him back, and I still do. In brutal honesty, I know that the wage of sin is death, so I should have been in the passenger seat of Fabe's Ford Taurus. I have done enough in my lifetime for my mom to have buried us both, but I am still here by grace. I have overcome feeling like God was angry with me, and now I am grateful that he did not give me what my sins deserve.

Journaling is still a crucial part of my self-care. When I am questioning my faith, it does help for me to be able to see God. I have seen God move in my life and I have been able to capture several of those moments in my journal. Here are more of my entries:

May 16, 2017 - For the first time ever, my coworkers coordinated a dinner party for my birthday. I have never had a dinner party, and I have not had a party for my birthday since my high school graduation. It was sort of a 2-in-1. My coworkers don't owe me a thing! I really hope they know how much I appreciate them.

July 15, 2017 - I met Barbara Corcoran and Laila Ali at an all-expense paid empowerment workshop in New York City today. The hotel is beautiful. In addition to trip expenses, my clothing and food was paid for. My parents, aunt, and uncle joined me. I appreciate their sacrifice; it was spur of the moment to purchase hotel and flight to NYC. Not to mention, we're in the heart of summer. It's been amazing so far! I constructed my first elevator pitch. It could definitely use some improvement.

August 21, 2017 – After one week of an orientation course, today is my first day of class as a Baylor University Graduate Student! The monthly court appearances prepared me for downtown's crazy, weekday traffic. Whenever I heard Baylor, the last thing that came to mind was diverse. I walked in to find a cohort that looks handpicked from the heart of Houston. I'm so excited about the diversity. I'm looking forward to our time together because I've never spent this much time with people who were this different than me. I can learn just as much from them as I can the professors.

April 06, 2018 - Over one year since my brother's murder and over 2 months since trial. I am feeling much more optimistic about life. Every day, I strive to be a victor, not a victim. All the glory and honor belong to God. I am so unworthy. I am not proud of me, but I am proud of the fact that God chose me. Social media has helped me connect with others. I have connected with another mother whose son was murdered just days before Fabian's 30th birthday party. The stories are so similar that it's unsettling. The social worker in me wanted to use Shulman skills during the call, but I couldn't think of one. I couldn't think of anything. I felt that mother's pain through the phone. I felt like God was forcing me to speak with my own mother, on February 19, 2017, when I had avoided her calls.

Although Tyler Green is incarcerated, the enemy is still busy. He has started the appeal process. I refuse to live in fear or misery. My mental health is my greatest priority because I have experienced so many mental attacks. Although I do not consume any medication on a regular basis (and never completed that psych eval), I have established relationships with professionals to discuss my headaches, triggers, emotions, and appropriate responses. I am very open about my brokenness. I have learned something from everyone I allowed to teach me something. Most of them were also broken. I pray that I have made my big brother proud. He definitely made me proud to be his little sister. I pray that God forgives me for questioning His power because I was in pain.

With the remainder of my life, I will serve God and His people. I am an advocate for many causes, but my heart tends to rest with those who have experienced victimization. In remembering one of the greatest advocates who ever lived, Martin Luther King, Jr., I have a dream that one day, the layers of stigma that rest on mental health within the African-American community will be removed. My goal is to collaborate with like-minded individuals to provide every service I needed and could not find when I considered giving up on life.

Lastly, I pray that God comforts the Green family. They were within arm's reach of us for a week during trial. While we were downtrodden, they filled the courtroom and lobby with smiles and laughter. We lost Fabian on Sunday February 19, 2017. Maybe they had not realized they had lost their son too.

> "Her freedom is attached to her ability to forgive" –
> Unknown

Appendix A

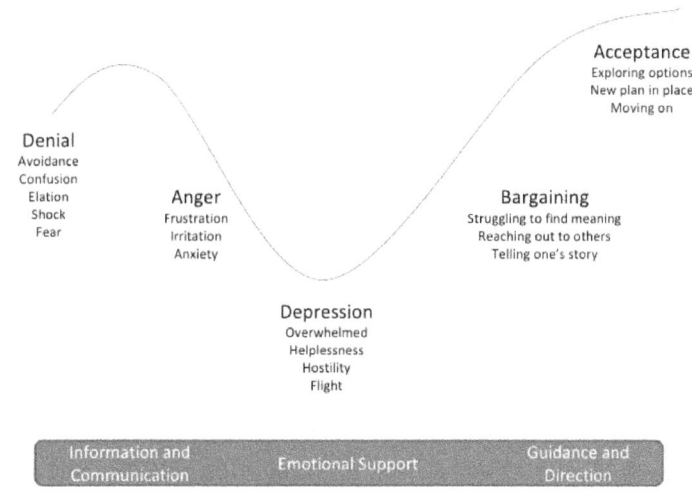

---

[3] The 5 Stages of Grief
https://grief.com/the-five-stages-of-grief/

Appendix B

Victim Impact Statement

The crime

On February 19, 2017, Tyler Green executed my brother. Afterwards, Tyler returned to record another episode of his life as usual (lying and hiding things), while my family and I were forced into lead roles of this horror movie. As details of this heinous crime unfold, they interrupt the stages of the grieving process; from knowing that the murderer left the scene in the car that he purchased from my brother to him taking backroads to flee the scene, and these backroads happen to be in the neighborhood where I reside. I knew my brother, his small frame, and unforgettable smile-& I would've never imagined him being the victim **of an execution.**

The Defendant

When I saw the news, although I was unsure as to who the murderer was at that time, I knew that law enforcement was searching for a monster. The aggravating circumstances of the execution imply that Tyler Green is a threat to the public, while his unwavering drug addiction proves that he is also a threat to himself. He placed a higher value on the prescription medication that he was feening for than my brother's life. If free, what would keep him from reoffending? The murderer has appeared before us for several days, with no signs of remorse. He has entered and exited the courtroom with an evil arrogance, inconsistent with his recent claim of self-defense.

The effect of the crime on the victim & victim's family

As a result of Tyler Green's malicious actions, my big brother, and my mom's only son is gone. All my life, I've heard her say to him "watch out for your sisters." Almost 1 year later, and I'm still trying to figure out who's supposed to do that now? The graveyard is filled with my brother's aspirations to attend culinary arts school, write and record music, and establish his own clothing line, just to name a few...

He'll never experience fatherhood or being a husband. Even the murderer mentioned his high-energy. Fabian was the light of our home, it's so dark without him. My family recently survived our first set of major holidays without him, and his birthday was barely two weeks ago. We spent Thanksgiving and Christmas at the graveyard, but Tyler Green mentioned having attended a New Year's party. To say the least, this murder was definitely unexpected; Fabian told me he'd be right back. As a result of Tyler's actions, we've missed countless days of school and work, attended grief counseling, and sought out additional victim services to cope with fear, anxiety, and depression. On behalf of the Smith Family, thank you for upholding the principles that our nation is founded upon. Thank you for Justice!

Rest in Heaven

Fabian "Fabe" Smith

January 16, 1988 ~ February 19, 2017

About the Author

Bianca's professional background includes criminal justice and human services. She currently serves as an advocate for justice and equity in health care. She was pushed into her purpose after the gruesome murder of her older brother. Bianca is passionate about increasing mental health awareness and acceptance.

She is a Master of Social Work candidate at Baylor University's Garland School of Social Work (Houston, TX). She also attended Sam Houston State University (Huntsville, TX) where she earned a Bachelor of Science in Criminal Justice (2012).

Bianca was raised in a family church and still considers weekly worship her favorite commitment. She also enjoys time with her family, traveling, and volunteer work. The author hopes this book will inspire you to be an advocate for yourself and for those who have been silenced by death or structural inequality.

"Don't allow tragedy to make you doubt what you know to be true, or people will doubt you!"
~Bianca Smith

Want to Connect?
Email: Bianca_Smith1@baylor.edu
Facebook: Bee Smith
Instagram: @findingfabe

www.ingramcontent.com/pod-product-compliance
Lightning Source LLC
LaVergne TN
LVHW051508070426
835507LV00022B/2993